AMID THE CULTURAL CHAOS

Are We Casualties or Conquerors?

James Perry

AMID THE CULTURAL CHAOS

Copyright © 2013 by James Perry

Published by: Theocentric Publishing Group
1069A Main St.
Chipley, Florida 32428
http://www.theocentricpublishing.com

All rights reserved. No part of this book may be reproduced or transmitted in any form or by any means without written permission of the author.

Unless otherwise noted, Scripture Quotations are from: The American Standard Version (ASV – 1901). It is in the public domain.

New King James Version, Scripture quotations marked (NKJV) are taken from the New King James Version. Copyright © 1982 by Thomas Nelson, Inc.

New Living Translation, Scripture quotations marked (NLT) are taken from the Holy Bible, New Living Translation, copyright © 1996, 2004, 2007 by Tyndale House Foundation.

New International Version, Scripture quotations marked (NIV) are taken from the Holy Bible, New International Version®, NIV®. Copyright © 1973, 1978, 1984 by Biblica, Inc.

J. B. Phillips, "The New Testament in Modern English", 1962 edition, published by HarperCollins.

Library of Congress Control Number: 2013956410

ISBN 9780985618186

DEDICATION

Keaton Lucas Barron is one of my Great Grandsons. When he was 2 ½ on August 29, 2012, he was attending a gymnastics class and unable to participate fully. His Mother had been concerned for a couple of weeks and had taken him to the Doctor who had given him some antibiotics. The Doctor was contacted once again and Keaton was brought in for some blood tests. The Doctor was gone for an extended period of time and when she returned she advised Keaton's mother to take him to the Children's Hospital right away because it appeared that he had Leukemia. The tests were done at the hospital and it was confirmed that Keaton had ALL. The recommended treatments that were needed began immediately.

ALL is also called Acute Lymphocytic Leukemia and Acute Lymphoid Leukemia. ALL is the most common type of cancer in children from 1 to 7 years old. ALL affects the blood cells and immune system. There are several ALL subtypes. The type of treatment you receive and your treatment outcome depend on your ALL subtype and individual risk factors. The overall survival statistic for children under 5 years of age with ALL is 90.8 percent, according to the National Cancer Institute. Most children with ALL are cured of their disease after treatment. (Source:

Acute Lymphoblastic Leukemia. Reviewed by Richard A. Larson, MD.)

Keaton has a great personality, is very courageous and has been very cooperative throughout his treatments. . In so many ways, he is a little hero and a champion. He will have to receive daily medication and return to the Hospital each month for maintenance treatment until he reaches 6 years of age.

I greatly admire this little one for his courage, confidence and cheerfulness. He has met each challenge with understanding and acceptance. Many have been and are praying for Keaton Barron that he will fully recover. My personal prayer is that the Sovereign God will continue to watch over this little lamb and that Keaton Barron will become a man of God who will make a positive difference Amid The Cultural Chaos. It is my joyous privilege to dedicate this book to my Great Grandson – Keaton Lucas Barron.

Foreword

The follower of Jesus Christ was never called to a lifestyle of leisure and detachment but to a life-commitment to activity and engagement. For the one who believes they lack capability for the task, the words of Jesus Christ to His disciples should resonate within us, namely, "Follow Me, I will make you fishers of men." He chose men from various backgrounds and varying capability for His kingdom work. For each one, the call first issued to Peter and Andrew echoed similarly for them: "Follow Me, I will make you..." As one thinks of that call, it becomes obvious that there are no valid excuses to be offered. Jesus Christ has declared that He will make His followers and servants into what He wants them to be. All that is required is for one to "immediately drop the nets" and follow.

As a youth, I remember the words of a stirring Hymn written by Frances Jane ("Fanny") Crosby in 1890, Victory Through Grace (this Hymn is now in the public domain). Note the powerful and challenging words:

> Conquering now and still to conquer,
> rideth a king in His might;
> Leading the host of all the faithful
> into the midst of the fight;
> See them with courage advancing,
> clad in their brilliant array,
> Shouting the name of their leader,
> hear them exultingly say:

Refrain:
Not to the strong is the battle,
Not to the swift is the race,
Yet to the true and the faithful
Vict'ry is promised through grace.

Conquering now and still to conquer,
who is this wonderful king?
Whence are the armies which He leadeth,
while of His glory they sing?
He is our Lord and Redeemer,
Savior and monarch divine;
They are the stars that forever bright
in His kingdom shall shine.

Conquering now and still to conquer,
Jesus, Thou ruler of all,
Thrones and their scepters all shall perish,
crowns and their splendor shall fall,
Yet shall the armies Thou leadest,
faithful and true to the last,
Find in Thy mansions eternal rest,
when their warfare is past.

Two passages of Scripture come to mind when reading this Hymn: First, Ecclesiastes 9:10-12, "Whatever your hand finds to do, do it with your might; for there is no work or device or knowledge or wisdom in the grave where you are going. I returned and saw under the sun that - The race is not to the swift, nor the battle to the strong, nor bread to the wise, nor riches to men of understanding, nor favor to men of skill; but time and chance happen to them all. For man also does not know his time:

Like fish taken in a cruel net, like birds caught in a snare, so the sons of men are snared in an evil time, when it falls suddenly upon them." The emphasis of the Hymn is verse 11, "the race is not to the swift, nor the battle to the strong." Second, Romans 8:35-37, "Who shall separate us from the love of Christ? Shall tribulation, or distress, or persecution, or famine, or nakedness, or peril, or sword? As it is written: For Your sake we are killed all day long; we are accounted as sheep for the slaughter. Yet in all these things we are more than conquerors through Him who loved us." The emphasis is verse 37, "we are more than conquerors through Him Who loved us."

A saying attributed to Saint Augustine is: "Pray as though everything depended on God. Work as though everything depended on you." This same truth should apply to one's level of engagement "Amid The Cultural Chaos." The task is formidable. The opposition is strong and unrelenting. The battle is not easy. For the follower of Christ, shrinking back or being detached is unacceptable. As one considers the dimensions and the paradigm of the culture, engagement is the necessary action. The encouragement and motivation should be similar to that of the Apollo 13 Crew, namely, "Failure Is Not An Option."

Words attributed to George Bernard Shaw can also be part of the vision and energy for the task at hand – "Some men see things as they are and say – Why? I dream of things that never were and say – Why not!" Rather than being focused on whether or not one will be successful, the focus should be whether or not I will serve faithfully. If one has any hesitation at this point, then more than likely there will be the experience of stumbling and faltering. One can and should ask the Lord who has issued His mandate to enable us to accomplish the assigned task well. If there is a sense of being unable to do or being inadequate for the task, then asking God for His help is basic. A guideline in asking is "if you believe and do not doubt". In James 1:5-7, "If any of you lacks wisdom, let him ask of God, who gives to all liberally and without reproach, and it will be given to him. But let him ask in faith, with no doubting, for he who doubts is like a wave of the sea driven and tossed by the wind. For let not that man suppose that he will receive anything from the Lord." The Message paraphrase is, "If you don't know what you're doing, pray to the Father. He loves to help. You'll get his help, and won't be condescended to when you ask for it. Ask boldly, believingly, without a second thought. People who worry their prayers are like wind-whipped waves. Don't think you're going to get anything from the Master that way..."

The chorus to the hymn, Loyalty To Christ, can serve as a victory hymn for the people of God. The words are:

> On to victory! On to victory!
> Cries our great commander, On!
> We'll move at His command,
> We'll soon possess the land,
> Through loyalty, loyalty,
> Yes, loyalty to Christ.

May we all be found faithful and zealous as we take our place in the Cultural Conflict and do what our Great Commander declares that will lead us on to Victory and Conquering in His Name.

May the following pages serve to be both instructive and encouraging as you make your commitment to be and do all that the Lord asks of you! God bless you as you become more engaged in the tremendous task at hand.

Table of Contents

1. Beginning a World and Life View 1
2. The Causes for Alternative Choices 17
3. The Redemptive Plan 33
4. Application of the Let Us to Us 47
5. The Church - Form and Function 65
6. A Functional Profile 81
7. Personal Engagement 95
8. The Risks of Personal Engagement 111
9. Intimidation (Bullying) 129
10. Being Factual or Fallacious 145
11. Living Credibly 165
12. Regret or Reward 181
13. Stirred and Focused 195
14. What's Next? 211

1. Beginning a World and Life View

When the Triune God determined to create the universe and to establish the world, the entire spectrum of what this world would be was firm in the mind of God. In His eternal plan, it was intended to be an *ex nihilo* creation of the planet earth. *Ex nihilo* is a Latin term meaning "from out of nothing." This is echoed in Hebrews 11:3, " By faith we understand that the worlds have been framed by the word of God, so that what is seen hath not been made out of things which appear." It's the idea expressed in Psalm 33:8-11, "Let all the earth fear Jehovah: Let all the inhabitants of the world stand in awe of him. For he spoke, and it was done; He commanded, and it stood fast. Jehovah brings the counsel of the nations to naught; He makes the thoughts of the peoples to be of no effect. The counsel of Jehovah stands fast for ever, The thoughts of his heart to all generations." In Romans 4:16-18, there is an important faith principle stated, "…God, who giveth life to the dead, and calls the things that are not, as though they were.…" Scholars take this to mean that the universe came into existence by divine command and was not assembled from preexisting matter or energy. God did not order materials from a Building and Supply establishment. He spoke, and it came into being.

When The Godhead decided to create Man, there were at least three major purposes that Man would have to fulfill. First, he would know the uniqueness of a perfect environment and culture in which he would exist and could enjoy. Second, he would know the perfect reality of daily fellowship and communion with his Creator. It was a time when he was immediately and instantly in the presence of God. This is apparent, when after The Fall, we read in Genesis 3:8, "And they heard the sound of the Lord God walking in the garden in the cool of the day, and Adam and his wife hid themselves from the presence of the Lord God among the trees of the garden." They had come to anticipate and desire being in the presence of God. But now, something had changed. Their innocence had been infiltrated and been destroyed. Something new was now part of their knowledge and experience, namely, sin. Third, Man would be a caretaker of The Earth that had been created. In Genesis 1:26-27, "And God said, Let us make man in our image, after our likeness: and let them have dominion over the fish of the sea, and over the birds of the heavens, and over the cattle, and over all the earth, and over every creeping thing that creepeth upon the earth. And God created man in his own image, in the image of God created he him; male and female created he them.."

Being made in the image of God is not in terms of physical attributes, but is in terms of character and nature. Man was given a soul that will never die. The image-factor is clarified in passages such as, Ephesians 4:24, "...put on the new man, that after God hath been created in righteousness and holiness of truth." Further amplification is given in Colossians 3:10, "...the new man, that is being renewed unto knowledge after the image of him that created him..." The renewal process takes place as II

Corinthians 5:17 (NKJV) is implemented and becomes the reality in man today, "...if anyone is in Christ, he is a new creation; old things have passed away; behold, all things have become new." As the "new creation" begins, so does the renewal process and image-factor wherein one is being renewed in (a) true righteousness, (b) true holiness, and (c) true knowledge.

The summary of the creation of Man is given in Genesis 2:15-17 (NKJV), "Then the Lord God took the man and put him in the Garden of Eden to tend and keep it. And the Lord God commanded the man, saying: Of every tree of the garden you may freely eat; but of the tree of the knowledge of good and evil you shall not eat, for in the day that you eat of it you shall surely die." The introduction of The Cultural Mandate is given in Genesis 1:28-30, "And God blessed them: and God said unto them, Be fruitful, and multiply, and replenish the earth, and subdue it; and have dominion over the fish of the sea, and over the birds of the heavens, and over every living thing that moves upon the earth. And God said, Behold, I have given you every herb yielding seed, which is upon the face of all the earth, and every tree, in which is the fruit of a tree yielding seed; to you it shall be for food: and to every beast of the earth, and to every bird of the heavens, and to everything that creeps upon the earth, wherein there is life, I have given every green herb for food: and it was so. ."

There is no indication of a time period between the creation of Man and the serpent's actions in the Garden of Eden that resulted in The Fall of Man. A moment came when God became displeased with the serpent's maneuvering and man's choice. Once man chose to listen to the serpent rather than to God, The Fall occurred. Why? In Genesis 3:22 (NKJV), the answer is given: "Then the Lord God said, Behold, the man has become like one of Us, to know good and evil. And now, lest he put out his hand and take also of the tree of life, and eat, and live forever therefore the Lord God sent him out of the Garden of Eden to till the ground from which he was taken. So He drove out the man; and He placed cherubim at the east of the Garden of Eden, and a flaming sword which turned every way, to guard the way to the tree of life." That one moment of Man's failure set in motion sin entering the perfect world, and death because of sin. It also set in motion a pattern of behavior that became a world and life view that was embraced within the expanding culture.

Man would now live *Amid The Cultural Chaos* where his choices would determine whether or not he would emerge as A Casualty or A Conqueror. What the response of man to the temptation by the serpent, and the ensuing consequences is stated in Romans 5:12-14 (NKJV), "Therefore, just as through one man sin entered the world, and death through sin, and thus death spread to all men, because all sinned. For until the law sin was in the world, but sin is not imputed when there is no law. Nevertheless death reigned from Adam to Moses, even over those who had not sinned according to the likeness of the transgression of Adam, who is a type of Him who was to come."

It would not be very long before God intervened in His creation because of the corruption that had quickly developed. We get a picture of this corruption and extent of cultural chaos in Genesis 6:1-8 where a description of what God observed and what the "let us" determined must take place. "And it came to pass, when men began to multiply on the face of the ground, and daughters were born unto them, that the sons of God saw the daughters of men that they were fair; and they took them wives of all that they chose. And Jehovah said, My spirit shall not strive with man forever, for that he also is flesh: yet shall his days be a hundred and twenty years. The Nephilim were in the earth in those days, and also after that, when the sons of God came unto the daughters of men, and they bore children to them: the same were the mighty men that were of old, the men of renown. And Jehovah saw that the wickedness of man was great in the earth, and that every imagination of the thoughts of his heart was only evil continually. And it repented Jehovah that he had made man on the earth, and it grieved him at his heart. And Jehovah said, I will destroy man whom I have created from the face of the ground; both man, and beast, and creeping things, and birds of the heavens; for it repenteth me that I have made them. But Noah found favor in the eyes of Jehovah."

It is difficult to conceive the full meaning of what was occurring so that "...God was grieved in His heart." In *Matthew Henry's Concise Commentary*, he observes: "God sees all the wickedness that is among the children of men; it cannot be hid from him now; and if it be not repented of, it shall be made known by him shortly. The wickedness of a people is great indeed, when noted sinners are men renowned among them. Very much sin was committed in all places, by all sorts of people. Any one might see that the wickedness of man was great: but God saw that every imagination, or purpose, of the thoughts of man's heart, was only evil continually. This was the bitter root, the corrupt spring. The heart was deceitful and desperately wicked; the principles were corrupt; the habits and dispositions evil. Their designs and devices were wicked. They did evil deliberately, contriving how to do mischief. There was no good among them."

As a means of both judging and cleansing the Earth, God sent rain and caused a Flood in accordance with His will. Jesus, a part of the "let us" determination, summarizes the reality of The Flood in Matthew 24:36-39 (NKJV), "...But as the days of Noah were, so also will the coming of the Son of Man be. For as in the days before the flood, they were eating and drinking, marrying and giving in marriage, until the day that Noah entered the ark, and did not know until the flood came and took them all away, so also will the coming of the Son of Man be." Matthew Henry adds: "God resolves to destroy man: the original word is very striking, 'I will wipe off man from the earth,' as dirt or filth is wiped off from a place which should be clean, and is thrown to the dunghill, the proper place for it. God speaks of man as his own creature, when he resolves upon his punishment...God speaks of resolution concerning men, after his Spirit had been long striving with them in vain. None are punished by the justice of God, but those who hate to be reformed by the grace of God."

After The Flood, there would come another occasion when God saw behavior that was not in accord with His will and was displeasing to Him. It occurs in Genesis 11. God is always observing the ways, the words and the deeds of those who inhabit His world. His purpose is for them to seek Him and to desire fellowship with Him. He wants them to love Him and to obey His precepts. The Fall allowed for the seed of sin to permeate mankind. The mind, emotion and will of man was more and more departing from God and His ways. Man, left to his devices, is just like man as seen by God in Genesis 6:5, "...the Lord saw that the wickedness of man was great in the earth, and that every intent of the thoughts of his heart was only evil continually." How far would man go? What would his imagination allow him to conceive? Collectively, what kinds of things would "the thoughts of his heart" consider and be willing to be in league with others of similar persuasion? Amid The Cultural Chaos of the twenty-first century, it is apparent that boundaries have been removed and there is no restraint to prevent anyone from approaching the slippery slope. The laws of the day, those which have been enacted, condone behavior that God has condemned. There seems to be no regard or any restraint for the life-style choices people are making in this day. It is more and more "like it was in the days of Noah..."

Note what mankind conceived and attempted to do in Genesis 11:1-9, "And the whole earth was of one language and of one speech. And it came to pass, as they journeyed east, that they found a plain in the land of Shinar; and they dwelt there. And they said one to another, Come, let us make brick, and burn them thoroughly. And they had brick for stone, and slime had they for mortar. And they said, Come, let us build us a city, and a tower, whose top may reach unto heaven, and let us make us a name; lest we be scattered abroad upon the face of the whole earth. And Jehovah came down to see the city and the tower, which the children of men builded. And Jehovah said, Behold, they are one people, and they have all one language; and this is what they begin to do: and now nothing will be withheld from them, which they purpose to do. Come, let us go down, and there confound their language, that they may not understand one another's speech. So Jehovah scattered them abroad from thence upon the face of all the earth: and they left off building the city. Therefore was the name of it called Babel; because Jehovah did there confound the language of all the earth: and from thence did Jehovah scatter them abroad upon the face of all the earth."

    Since The Fall of Man in the Garden, the culture began to be marred and scarred. The culture became more creative as it unleashed its imagination and thoughts. Did they know there was an Eternal God? Were they aware of His requirements and standards? Did they care that there was a culture available to them that would be marked by true knowledge, righteousness and holiness? Are there ways by which they could have and should have known that God existed and was The Creator? Could they observe that which David observed when he wrote in Psalm 19:1-4 (NKJV), "The heavens declare the glory of God; and the firmament shows His handiwork. Day unto day utters speech, and night unto night reveals knowledge. There is no speech nor language where their voice is not heard. Their line has gone out through all the earth and their words to the end of the world."? The answer to these rhetorical questions is, "Yes!" Romans 1:18-22 (NKJV) addresses this point precisely. "For the wrath of God is revealed from heaven against all ungodliness and unrighteousness of men, who suppress the truth in unrighteousness, because what may be known of God is manifest in them, for God has shown it to them. For since the creation of the world His invisible attributes are clearly seen, being understood by the things that are made, even His eternal power and Godhead, so that they are without excuse, because, although they knew God, they did not glorify Him as God, nor were thankful, but became futile in their thoughts, and their foolish hearts were darkened. Professing to be wise, they became fools, and changed the glory of the incorruptible God into an image made like corruptible man--and birds and four-footed animals and creeping things."

Deliberate choices by man and mankind will result in deliberate consequences. (1) In the Garden of Eden (Genesis 3), Man lost his perfect environment and culture, along with the reality of God coming in the evening walking amidst His Creation and with His creatures. Man was banished from that which was perfect into a world unknown to him. He would know sweat, toil, pain and failure. (2) When the human race became more and more perverse, and "the thoughts of man was only evil continually" (Genesis 6), a Flood was sent by God to judge, purge, and cleanse the earth. Even though the Lord spared Noah and his family, the seeds of sin were still embedded in Man. It would not be too long before man and mankind's imagination would once again be the occasion of a behavior that was repulsive and could not be allowed. (3) Mankind allowed itself to think and plan (Genesis 11). They arrive at a decision and plan, namely, "…let us build ourselves a city, and (let us build) a tower whose top is in the heavens; let us make a name for ourselves…" Notice a blatant change that is occurring at this juncture. The "let us" of the Godhead is being supplanted by the "let us" of a depraved and narcissistic generation. Their focus was, "let us make a name for ourselves." The idea of the Glory of God was not a part of their consciousness. They had become self-centered and self-absorbed. The issue for them was in terms of what they can do so that they will be remembered and their name will be both historically and significantly remembered. In a way, they achieved their goal, but not in the manner they had imagined or desired.

In the 21st Century, a Christian and Biblical Worldview is indispensible. There are many intrusions into one's thinking that flow from a decadent and eroding culture. An article published by Focus on the Family asks, "What's a Christian Worldview?" by Del Tackett.. The article states: "A recent nationwide survey completed by the Barna Research Group determined that only 4 percent of Americans had a "biblical" worldview. When George

Barna, who has researched cultural trends and the Christian Church since 1984, looked at the "born- again" believers in America, the results were a dismal 9 percent..."Barna's survey also connected an individual's worldview with his or her moral beliefs and actions. Barna says, "Although most people own a Bible and know some of its content, our research found that most Americans have little idea how to integrate core biblical principles to form a unified and meaningful response to the challenges and opportunities of life. A biblical worldview is based on the infallible Word of God. When you believe the Bible is entirely true, then you allow it to be the foundation of everything you say and do. That means, for instance, you take seriously the mandate in Romans 13 to honor the governing authorities by researching the candidates and issues, making voting a priority...Do you have a biblical worldview? Answer the following questions, based on claims found in the Bible and which George Barna used in his survey: Do absolute moral truths exist? Is absolute truth defined by the Bible? Did Jesus Christ live a sinless life? Is God the all-powerful and all-knowing Creator of the universe, and does He still rule it today? Is salvation a gift from God that cannot be earned? Is Satan real? Does a Christian have a responsibility to share his or her faith in Christ with other people? Is the Bible accurate in all of its teachings?

"Did you answer yes to these? Only 9 percent of "born-again" believers did. But what's more important than your replying yes to these questions is whether your life shows it. Granted, we are all sinners and fall short, but most of our gut reactions will reflect what we deep-down, honest-to-goodness believe to be real and true....Here is the big problem. Non-biblical worldview ideas don't just sit in a book somewhere waiting for people to examine them. They bombard us constantly from television, film, music, newspapers, magazines, books and academia...Because we live in a selfish, fallen world, these ideas seductively appeal to the desires of our flesh, and we often end up incorporating them into our personal worldview. Sadly, we often do this without even knowing it...If we don't really believe the truth of God and live it, then our witness will be confusing and misleading. Most of us go through life not recognizing that our personal worldviews have been deeply affected by the world. Through the media and other influences, the secularized American view of history, law, politics, science, God and man affects our thinking more than we realize. We then are taken "captive through hollow and deceptive philosophy, which depends on human tradition and the basic principles of this world rather than on Christ" (Colossians 2:8). However, by diligently learning, applying and trusting God's truths in every area of our lives — whether it's watching a movie, communicating with our spouses, raising our children or working at the office — we can begin to develop a deep comprehensive faith that will stand against the unrelenting tide of our culture's non-biblical ideas. If we capture and embrace more of God's worldview and trust it with unwavering faith, then we begin to make the right decisions and form the appropriate responses to questions on abortion, same- sex marriage, cloning, stem-cell research and even media choices. Because, in the end, it is our decisions and actions that reveal what we really believe. Do not conform any longer to the pattern of this world, but be transformed by the renewing of your mind" (Romans 12:2)."

Having a Biblical and Christian worldview involves more than just a statement that one is a Christian or a believer. It necessitates knowing what one believes and why one believes it. There are many websites and books that make statements about Apologetics and what it means. A very trite summary of a worldview and apologetics is how one offers a defense of the faith. What does one offer and how does one defend the things one believes and proclaims? One submitted statement is" "Apologetics is the branch of Christianity that deals with the defense and establishment of the Christian faith. Christian Apologetics is something every true believer should be involved in, even if it is only a little." The Biblical foundation for that statement is cited in I Peter 3:15-16, "But sanctify the Lord God in your hearts, and always be ready to give a defense to everyone who asks you a reason for the hope that is in you, with meekness and fear; having a good conscience, that when they defame you as evildoers, those who revile your good conduct in Christ may be ashamed." The Message Paraphrase of verse 15 is, "Through thick and thin, keep your hearts at attention, in adoration before Christ, your Master. Be ready to speak up and tell anyone who asks why you're living the way you are, and always with the utmost courtesy."

FOR THOUGHT AND REFLECTION:

How would you define and state your worldview?

If a Muslim asked you to state why your God is to be preferred to their god, what would you say? How would you defend your belief in the one true God?

If a child asked you about what they should believe and why, what would you say to the child? What verses in the Bible would you use?

If an Atheist challenged the things you say you believe and was not interested in what the Bible states, is there a way to communicate the Gospel to him/her? How? In what way?

If a person on their death-bed is asked by you, "Why should God let you into His heaven?" and their reply was because they had lived a good life and had attended church regularly and given what they could, would you accept that as being a credible profession of faith? Why? Why not? What would you say is necessary for one to believe and be saved?

Who is responsible for establishing a Biblical and Christian Worldview and championing it? A denomination? A prominent church leader? A religious organization? You? Explain your answer and rationale.

Did the Berean believers in Acts 17 accept the worldview of Paul and the other Apostles as the standard and absolute? What did the worldview of the Apostles have as its foundation? How did the Bereans determine it? What should you do to arrive at a Biblical and Christian worldview?

Do you think Adam and Eve had a worldview while they were in the Garden of Eden? If so, what do you think it was? What happened to cause them to jettison the initial worldview for a lesser alternative? What was at the center of their choice?

As you live Amid The Cultural Chaos of these time, will you emerge as A Casualty or as A Conqueror? What do you need to do to become A Conqueror? (See: Romans 8:31-39 for your answer).

"Reverently respect God, your God,
serve him, hold tight to him,
back up your promises with the authority of his name.
He's your praise!
He's your God!"
Deuteronomy 10:20-21 (The Message)

2. The Causes for Alternative Choices

The choice made by Adam and Eve for the alternative worldview to that which had been established by the Godhead (the "let us") is clearly stated in Genesis 3:1-8. The process of moving from a God-view to an alternative view occurs subtly but purposefully. The text reads: "Now the serpent was more cunning than any beast of the field which the Lord God had made. And he said to the woman, Has God indeed said, you shall not eat of every tree of the garden? And the woman said to the serpent, we may eat the fruit of the trees of the garden; but of the fruit of the tree which is in the midst of the garden, God has said, You shall not eat it, nor shall you touch it, lest you die. Then the serpent said to the woman, you will not surely die. For God knows that in the day you eat of it your eyes will be opened and you will be like God, knowing good and evil. So when the woman saw that the tree was good for food, that it was pleasant to the eyes, and a tree desirable to make one wise, she took of its fruit and ate. She also gave to her husband with her, and he ate. Then the eyes of both of them were opened, and they knew that they were naked; and they sewed fig leaves together and made themselves coverings." The key to the serpent's approach is: "...in the day you eat of it your eyes will be opened, and you will be like God..." What a moment? You can make the choice to be more than what you are and be more than you ever imagined. No, it is a moment that should be ignored! What an opportunity?

To think, one can be "like God" and all one has to do is to partake of that which has been forbidden by God? No, it is an opportunity that must be avoided at all costs!

Why did the serpent suggest to Adam and Eve that they partake of that which was forbidden by God? What occasioned this moment and suggestion of a godless alternative? Is it possible that Adam and Eve had walked passed the Tree of the Knowledge of Good and Evil, and each time they did so, the fruit of it looked more luscious and desirable? Is it possible that they mused between themselves and wondered why it had to be off-limits to them? Is it likely that the serpent, seeing this routine and behavior of Adam and Eve, used their musings and wonderment to his advantage? Would the serpent make his move and endeavor to gain the advantage by nudging them to act upon their desires? Why is this a likely scenario of how this occurred and what took place? There are two passages that provide us with insight in this regard. The first is James 1:13-15, "Let no one say when he is tempted, I am tempted by God; for God cannot be tempted by evil, nor does He Himself tempt anyone. But each one is tempted when he is drawn away by his own desires and enticed. Then, when desire has conceived, it gives birth to sin; and sin, when it is full-grown, brings forth death." The statement is clear, namely, "...each one is tempted when he is drawn away by his own desires and enticed..." The second text is Psalm 1:1 that demonstrates the process by which the temptation gradually becomes the reality: "Blessed is the man who walks not in the counsel of the ungodly, nor stands in the path of sinners, nor sits in the seat of the scornful." The process is apparent. (1) The individual begins to allow for an ungodly consideration, namely, thinking about that which God has forbidden. (2) All too soon, it becomes easier to stand in the vicinity where one should not be and gaze upon that which God has forbidden. (3) Permitting a shift in terms of one's comfort zone by sitting down and giving viable consideration to that which God has forbidden. This now becomes a point of personal vulnerability. It is at a point of vulnerability when the tempter usually enters and nudges one to change a Godly worldview and value system for one that allows for a narcissistic fulfillment.

Note the serpent's strategy and approach. He uses a series of questions and suggestions that are aimed at the point of their greatest vulnerability and weakness. The Message Paraphrase of Genesis 3:1-7 is both earthy and succinct: "The serpent was clever, more clever than any wild animal God had made. He spoke to the Woman: Do I understand that God told you not to eat from any tree in the garden? The Woman said to the serpent, Not at all. We can eat from the trees in the garden. It's only about the tree in the middle of the garden that God said, Don't eat from it; don't even touch it or you'll die. The serpent told the Woman, You won't die. God knows that the moment you eat from that tree, you'll see what's really going on. You'll be just like God, knowing everything, ranging all the way from good to evil. When the Woman saw that the tree looked like good eating and realized what she would get out of it - she'd know everything! - She took and ate the fruit and then gave some to her husband,

and he ate. Immediately the two of them did see what's really going on and saw themselves naked! "They sewed fig leaves together as makeshift clothes for themselves." The enemy is a clever strategist. He knew more about Adam and Eve than they knew about themselves. He knew the right approach to achieve his goal and purpose in their lives and he succeeded.

The serpent knew what he was achieving. This was his first step in bringing about the cultural chaos that prevails to this day. He had attempted to do for himself in eternity past that which he enticed Eve and then Adam to do in their present. He already knew the end result. He was undaunted and unhesitant. He boldly and brazenly entered into the Garden and their lives to achieve through them that which he had failed to achieve for himself. In Isaiah 14:12-15, we see the attempt and effort of the one who became the serpent: "How you are fallen from heaven, O Lucifer, son of the morning! How you are cut down to the ground...For you have said in your heart: I will ascend into heaven, I will exalt my throne above the stars of God; I will also sit on the mount of the congregation...I will ascend above the heights of the clouds, I will be like the Most High. Yet you shall be brought down to Sheol, to the lowest depths of the Pit." Even though he knew the failure of such an ambition, the serpent came to Adam and Eve with his lie and persuaded them that wrong would be right. All they had to do was to accept his suggestion and godless alternative. His lie materialized into their disobedience and being removed and barred from the Garden of Eden from that point onward. Adam and Eve had chosen to become casualties rather than conquerors when they succumbed to the serpent's wily ways.

Note his crafty and cunning approach. (1) Did God really say and mean that you could not eat from any tree in the garden? The woman's reply was quick and accurate. Oh, no! There is only one tree in the midst of the Garden which is off-limits to us. That one, God said, if you touch it and/or eat it – you will die! (2) The serpent was just as quick with his response. He states his alternative to what God has clearly stated and defined. The serpent says, essentially, that isn't true. The only reason God wants you to believe and remember that prohibition is to keep your eyes from being opened and your knowledge base being expanded. God knows that you will know what He knows. You will be like God and know the distinction between good and evil. (3) It is at this point that the woman decides to re-evaluate her God-given worldview and reassess her God-given core values. She permits herself to look at the luscious fruit on the tree and saw that it was very appealing. She was led to believe that her intelligence and knowledge base could be more than it was and she could be wiser and more knowledgeable. What should she do at this moment? What decision should be made? As she pondered her choices, she decided to take that fruit and to eat it. (4) She became an emissary for the alternative world and life view by suggesting to her husband that he could benefit by trying a piece of the fruit from the off-limits tree. So she gave him a piece of the fruit, and he ate it as well. (5) Instantaneously, they had a new experience and awareness. Their innocence was sacrificed as they realized they were both naked. They decided they should have some form of covering for their bodies. They took some leaves and knit them together so their bodies would be modestly covered. (6) All is well until the regular meeting time with God arrives and He comes on the scene during the evening hour. Ashamedly and/or fearfully, their first instinct was to hide from God. The key to the serpent's approach is: "…in the day you eat of it your eyes will be opened, and you will be like God…" Yielding to the cunning approach of the serpent had an immediate impact in and for their lives, namely, interrupting the fellowship they had been having with God on a daily basis. It will always be the case. It was true then and continues to be true today. If one fails to follow God's Word and walk in His ways, the tendency and action will be to try to hide from Him and to cover-up what one has done.

A basic truth one needs to remember about the enemy, the serpent, is that he is a liar. In John 8:43-44, Jesus identifies and defines who and what he is and does: "Why do you not understand My speech? Because you are not able to listen to My word. You are of your father the devil, and the desires of your father you want to do. He was a murderer from the beginning, and does not stand in the truth, because there is no truth in him. When he speaks a lie, he speaks from his own resources, for he is a liar and the father of it." The words of Jesus versus the words of the devil is the same scenario as in the Garden of Eden. Our human choice is between God's Word or the serpent's alternative. It is a life and death choice one must make. Believing the word of Jesus is eternal life and believing the word of the devil is eternal death. This is the battleground and line of engagement that each one experiences. The choice must be made – the Godly world and life view or the devil's godless substitute and alternative.

In choosing the godly world and life view does not mean one will be exempt from the enemy's tactics or ambitions. There is a cautionary word given to all who choose to follow Christ. The statement, "to be forewarned is to be forearmed" is relevant. The words of I John 2:14-17 must be evidenced and practiced in one's life: "I have written to you, fathers, because you have known Him who is from the beginning. I have written to you, young men, because you are strong, and the word of God abides in you, and you have overcome the wicked one. Do not love the world or the things in the world. If anyone loves the world, the love of the Father is not in him. For all that is in the world--the lust of the flesh, the lust of the eyes, and the pride of life is not of the Father but is of the world. And the world is passing away, and the lust of it; but he who does the will of God abides forever." The words are directed to believers, namely, "I have written to you, fathers, because you have known Him who is from the beginning. I have written to you, young men, because you are strong, and the word of God abides in you, and you have overcome the wicked one." The cautionary word is to the end that no child of God should allow himself/herself to walk, stand, or sit in the place of wrongdoing and temptation. Such a place is not the Garden of God, but the field of the enemy. In his field, there will be many temptations and enticements. One must exercise vigilance and discipline by avoiding that place and remaining close to the Garden and ways of God.

Even when one does, the temptation to forsake the way and purpose of God will come. This is exactly what occurred in the life of Jesus Christ. Matthew 4:1-11 records: "Then Jesus was led up by the Spirit into the wilderness to be tempted by the devil. And when He had fasted forty days and forty nights, afterward He was hungry. Now when the tempter came to Him, he said, If You are the Son of God, command that these stones become bread. But He answered and said, It is written, Man shall not live by bread alone, but by every word that proceeds from the mouth of God. Then the devil took Him up into the holy city, set Him on the pinnacle of the temple, and said to Him, If You are the Son of God, throw Yourself down. For it is written: He shall give His angels charge over you, and, In their hands they shall bear you up, Lest you dash your foot against a stone. Jesus said to him, It is written again, You shall not tempt the Lord your God. Again, the devil took Him up on an exceedingly high mountain, and showed Him all the kingdoms of the world and their glory. And he said to Him, All these things I will give You if You will fall down and worship me. Then Jesus said to him, Away with you, Satan! For it is written, You shall worship the Lord your God, and Him only you shall serve. Then the devil left Him, and behold, angels came and ministered to Him."

One must always be aware of and avoid the "if" of the enemy. It is his tactic to cause one to doubt and to consider godless alternative directions and life choices. This was the approach he used with Jesus Christ and it will be similar to the approach he will use with anyone else. When the devil comes to Jesus, his first question deals with the deity of Christ. It is not stated as a proposition but as a supposition. The following is the devil's approach: (1) "IF" You are the Son of God, You should be able to do anything at any time that You choose to do. The devil's hope and goal is that Jesus Christ might consider the false premise and think about the supposition. It would be a simple act, according to the devil. You're hungry and no food is available. However, there are stones everywhere. Command one or more of these stones to become bread. By doing so, your hunger needs can be met and your physical strength restored. The devil is not concerned about preserving the physical strength of Jesus Christ but undermining His spiritual commitment, discipline and strength. It is the devil's subtle attempt to get Jesus Christ to reevaluate His core values and Godly worldview to the self-serving and narcissistic alternative. Obviously, Jesus could have given the command to the stones and they would become bread. However, Jesus has a higher calling and standard. He states it clearly and forthrightly, "It is written, Man shall not live by bread alone, but by every word that proceeds from the mouth of God." Jesus Christ appealed to the revealed and written Word of God as He answered with the words of Deuteronomy 8:3, "So He humbled you, allowed you to hunger, and fed you with manna which you did not know nor did your fathers know, that He might make you know that man shall not live by bread alone; but man lives by every word that proceeds from the mouth of the Lord."

The devil is undaunted and unstoppable. He had another supposition for Jesus to consider. Jesus is brought to the pinnacle of the Temple in the Holy City and the devil says to Him: (2) "IF You are the Son of God, throw Yourself down." The idea is, IF You are all that You claim to be, and IF You have come from where You claim to have come, then You should be able to be unharmed and uninjured IF you approve my alternative for Your life. The devil is clever enough and cunning enough so that he will even quote some Scriptural statements. In this instance, he attempts his paraphrase by saying to Jesus: You do believe that God "...shall give His angels charge over you, and, in their hands they shall bear you up, lest you dash your foot against a stone." The devil is notorious for his misquotes of Scripture. The exact quote is from Psalm 91:11-12, "For He shall give His angels charge over you, to keep you in all your ways. In their hands they shall bear you up, lest you dash your foot against a stone." What has the devil chosen to omit? Why do you think he omitted it? How important is the omitted phrase for Jesus Christ? How important is it for you? The omitted phrase is: "To keep you in all your ways." The safest place one can be is when one's ways are God's ways. It reinforces the words of Proverbs 3:5-7, "Trust in the Lord with all your heart, and lean not on your own understanding; In all your ways acknowledge Him, and He shall direct your paths. Do not be wise in your own eyes; Fear the Lord and depart from evil." The directive is clear. "In all your ways acknowledge Him is unequivocal. It says what it means and means what it says. "In all your ways" does not allow for any alternative or revision. The answer of Jesus to the devil is a statement in Deuteronomy 6:14-16, "You shall not go after other gods, the gods of the peoples who are all around you…lest the anger of the Lord your God be aroused against you and destroy you from the face of the earth. You shall not tempt the Lord your God…"

Being undaunted and untiring, the devil is relentless in his efforts to thwart God's plan and will for His world. The devil wants his alternative to prevail whatever the effort and whatever the cost. The next effort of the devil in the life of Jesus Christ is to take Him up to a high mountain. He wants Jesus to look at all the kingdoms of the world, all their glory, all their appeal, and all their desirability. In an almost desperate appeal, the devil strips away his subtlety and asserts his one last effort with Jesus. (3) "All these things I will give You IF You will fall down and worship me." The devil overlooks the fact that Jesus was a member of the "Let Us" Godhead Who made a decision to create a universe and world. The devil does not own it and cannot give away what is not his to give. It's almost as though Jesus brushes aside this third and futile attempt of the devil. It is terse and direct: "Away with you, Satan!" Jesus then appeals to the overall teaching of Deuteronomy 6 and 8 by saying: "You shall worship the Lord your God, and Him only you shall serve."

The important Lessons one should learn and embrace are: Lesson (a) know the teaching of the Word of God. Not what you think it says, but what you know with certainty it does say.

Lesson (b) acknowledge God and His Word in and for all areas of one's life without exception. Lesson (c) never attempt to resist temptation on the basis of human intellect or logic. This is not an exercise to try in a human effort to outwit the devil. The issue is clear. One must stand on the promises of God. One must use God's Word and state it boldly and precisely. With the belief and commitment of the Psalmist, one must believe and implement Psalm 28:7, "The Lord is my strength and my shield; my heart trusted in Him, and I am helped; therefore my heart greatly rejoices, And with my song I will praise Him." When this is one's choice and is uncompromised, one will experience what Jesus knew: "Then the devil left Him, and behold, angels came and ministered to Him."

One other truth that needs to be remembered at this point is stated in I Corinthians 10:12-13, "Therefore let him who thinks he stands take heed lest he fall. No temptation has overtaken you except such as is common to man; but God is faithful, who will not allow you to be tempted beyond what you are able, but with the temptation will also make the way of escape, that you may be able to bear it." Temptations will come at different times and in various ways. The devil is relentless in his desire to bring about the fall of as many as he can. We should remember what we are instructed in Ephesians 6:11-18, "Put on the whole armor of God, that you may be able to stand against the wiles of the devil. For we do not wrestle against flesh and blood, but against principalities, against powers, against the rulers of the darkness of this age, against spiritual hosts of wickedness in the heavenly places. Therefore take up the whole armor of God, that you may be able to withstand in the evil day, and having done all, to stand. Stand therefore, having girded your waist with truth, having put on the breastplate of righteousness, and having shod your feet with the preparation of the gospel of peace; above all, taking the shield of faith with which you will be able to quench all the fiery darts of the wicked one. And take the helmet of salvation, and the sword of the Spirit, which is the word of God; praying always with all prayer and supplication in the Spirit, being watchful to this end with all perseverance and supplication for all the saints." We are instructed and warned about "all the fiery darts of the wicked one" and to be "watchful to the end with all perseverance and supplication." The devil's efforts *Amid The Cultural Chaos* are ongoing and he is relentless. He wants you to be a casualty rather than a conqueror. Resist steadfastly the alternative ways and proposals of the devil and make the deliberate choice that God's way is the only way for you. In Christ alone, we have our victory and sufficiency. We do not need to be causalities. In Christ, we are to be conquerors. We are safe and secure in Him, and rest securely and safely in the hollow of His protective hand.

FOR THOUGHT AND REFLECTION:

What do you consider to be the best way to resist Temptation?

Do you subscribe to the school that espouses, "I Talk Back To The Devil"? If so, what exactly does that mean?

What is the time when Temptation seems to be the greatest in one's life? When you are weary? When you are under some physical stress or tension? When personal needs are great and your personal resources are minimum? When you are sorrowing or grieving? When there is something you want and begin to obsess that you have to have it?

If/When you yield to temptation, what should you do and when should you do it?

Does delay in dealing with temptation become beneficial or detrimental in terms of your life and interpersonal relationships? (Read Psalm 32 and Psalm 51 to assist you with your answer). Is your "knee-jerk" reaction and response to deny what you have done? Will this prove to be helpful if you desire to walk with the Lord and in His ways?

If you confess your temptations and sins to the Lord, what is He faithful to do in your behalf? Share a Scripture Reference with your response.

What Biblical character is a classic example of one who attempted to ignore his yielding to temptation? How far was he willing to go to cover-up his transgression? Read II Samuel 11 to assist you with your answer.

Once David came to his senses and knew he had to acknowledge the temptation and transgression, how intense was that Confession and seeking for Restoration? Once again, read both Psalm 32 and Psalm 51 to assist you with your answer.

"Blessed is the man who perseveres under trial, because when he has stood the test, he will receive the crown of life that God has promised to those who love him. When tempted, no one should say, "God is tempting me." For God cannot be tempted by evil, nor does he tempt anyone; but each one is tempted when, by his own evil desire, he is dragged away and enticed. Then, after desire has conceived, it gives birth to sin; and sin, when it is full-grown, gives birth to death. Don't be deceived, my dear brothers."

James 1:12-16 (NIV)

3. The Redemptive Plan

When the triune Godhead created the universe, world and man, it set in motion the eternal plan. Nothing that had occurred or would occur caught God by surprise. He knew that man would disobey and sin. The Godhead determined that mankind would need a means for redemption. Part of the "Let Us" discussion and plan included the provision of a Redeemer and Redemption. One learns this from I Peter 1:17-21, "And if you call on the Father, who without partiality judges according to each one's work, conduct yourselves throughout the time of your stay here in fear; knowing that you were not redeemed with corruptible things, like silver or gold, from your aimless conduct received by tradition from your fathers, but with the precious blood of Christ, as of a lamb without blemish and without spot. He indeed was foreordained before the foundation of the world, but was manifest in these last times for you who through Him believe in God, who raised Him from the dead and gave Him glory, so that your faith and hope are in God." Verse 20 is clear when it states: "...before the foundation of the world..." this redemptive plan was established and set in motion. Jesus employed this phrase in His High Priestly Prayer in John 17:24, "Father, I desire that they also whom You gave Me may be with Me where I am, that they may behold My glory which You have given Me; for You loved Me before the foundation of the world." It is also used by the Apostle Paul in Ephesians 1:4-5, "...just as

He chose us in Him before the foundation of the world, that we should be holy and without blame before Him in love, having predestined us to adoption as sons by Jesus Christ to Himself, according to the good pleasure of His will."

Scripture is replete with this plan of and for redemption. It is indicated in Genesis 3:14-15, "So the Lord God said to the serpent: Because you have done this, you are cursed more than all cattle, and more than every beast of the field; on your belly you shall go, and you shall eat dust all the days of your life. And I will put enmity between you and the woman, and between your seed and her Seed; He shall bruise your head, and you shall bruise His heel." What is the issue here? What is the basis for both the declaration and impending judgment regarding the serpent? In Genesis 3:4-5, "Then the serpent said to the woman, you will not surely die. For God knows that in the day you eat of it your eyes will be opened and you will be like God, knowing good and evil." Based upon this text, there are at least three credible factors to be considered: (1) The serpent tempts the woman to be disobedient to God; (2) the serpent attempts to demote God by calling Him *Elohim* rather than *Yahweh Elohim*; and (3) the serpent infers that God is a liar when he states, "No, you will not die."

The serpent knows his own character very well. He knows what he has done in eternity past and is aware of what will occur in eternity future. What are some of the characteristics of the serpent? In Isaiah 14:12-15, there is a clear revealing of that which motivates and is the driving force of the serpent. It is summed up in the five "I wills" regarding Lucifer. "How you are fallen from heaven, O Lucifer, son of the morning! How you are cut down to the ground, you who weakened the nations!" The devil's personal ambition and goal is clear, (1) I will ascend into heaven! (2) I will exalt my throne above the stars of God! (3) I will also sit on the mount of the congregation on the farthest sides of the north! (4) I will ascend above the heights of the clouds! (5) I will be like the Most High! The Word of God states the ignored fact: "Yet you shall be brought down to Sheol, to the lowest depths of the Pit." Obviously, it addresses his ego-driven goal and his pride as he sought to achieve it. The serpent ignores this pending judgment for himself and tempts all to follow his lofty estimation of himself. He wants all to be inflated by one's ego and given to being dominated by one's pride. Part of this effort is to have one ignore Scripture, especially any declaration similar to Proverbs 16:18, "Pride goes before destruction and a haughty spirit before a fall."

The fact is that the serpent (also known by the names Lucifer, Satan, Devil) proves his relentlessness as he purposes to disrupt or thwart God's redemptive plan. One gets the sense of this determination in passages such as Matthew 4:1-11, the temptation of Jesus Christ in the wilderness, and in Jude 9, "Yet Michael the archangel, in contending with the devil, when he disputed about the body of Moses..." When temptations increase in intensity, one should remind himself/herself of the faithfulness of God to guard and protect His own. It echoes the reassuring words of Psalm 91:10-12, "No evil shall befall you, nor shall any plague come near your dwelling; for He shall give His angels charge over you, to keep you in all your ways. In their hands they shall bear you up, lest you dash your foot against a stone." It is imperative that one remembers what Redemption is and what it has accomplished, namely, one's deliverance from bondage and the deceptions of the evil one.

Redemption is summarized in Ephesians 1:7-8, "In him we have redemption through his blood, the forgiveness of sins, in accordance with the riches of God's grace that he lavished on us with all wisdom and understanding. And he made known to us the mystery of his will according to his good pleasure, which he purposed in Christ..." One's condition before redemption was being dead in trespasses and sin; enslaved by Satan's designs and whims. However, redemption resulted in one being purchased from slavery and realizing the scope and benefit of deliverance, rescue, and salvation. It included the realization that a cost was involved, namely, a blood sacrifice to achieve atonement and redemption. It includes an understanding of Hebrews 9:22, "...without shedding of blood there is no remission..." It incorporates also the knowledge of what and Who that sacrifice was in order that remission and redemption would occur. Hebrews 10:10 identifies that sacrifice: "...we have been sanctified through the offering of the body of Jesus Christ once for all."

Ephesians 1:7-8 included two actions that have taken place: In Christ we have (1) redemption through His blood, and (2) the forgiveness of sins. It is all on the basis of the riches of

God's grace. The "forgiveness of sins" should have a significant application in one's life. It is vital that one learn the basis and principle of forgiveness, as well as the practice of forgiveness. Following The Lord's Prayer, Jesus makes the following declaration in Matthew 6:14-15, "For if you forgive men their trespasses, your heavenly Father will also forgive you. But if you do not forgive men their trespasses, neither will your Father forgive your trespasses." The practice of forgiveness becomes a front and center issue for every professing follower of Jesus Christ.

There is an interesting presentation in a book by Ken Sande, A Biblical Guide To Resolving Personal Conflict, on page 209. It comes under the heading, "The Four Promises Of Forgiveness, powered by: Hebrews 9:21-22, "And in the same way he sprinkled with blood both the tent and all the vessels used in worship. Indeed, under the law almost everything is purified with blood, and without the shedding of blood there is no forgiveness of sins." The general application comes under a subheading, Forgiveness May Be Described As A Decision To Make Four Promises: (1) I will not dwell on this incident; (2) I will not bring up this incident again and use it against you; (3) I will not talk to others about this incident; (4) I will not let this incident stand between us or hinder our personal relationship."

The author continues: "By making and keeping these promises, you can tear down the walls that stand between you and your offender. You promise not to dwell on or brood over the problem or punish by holding the person at a distance. You clear the way for your relationship to develop unhindered by memories of past wrongs. This is exactly what God does for us, and what he calls us to do for others." According to the "Let Us" plan for the "new creation," II Corinthians 5:18-20, reconciliation is to be one's understanding and regular practice. The text states: "Now all things are of God, who has reconciled us to Himself through Jesus Christ, and has given us the ministry of reconciliation, that is, that God was in Christ reconciling the world to Himself, not imputing their trespasses to them, and has committed to us the word of reconciliation. Now then, we are ambassadors for Christ, as though God were pleading through us: we implore you on Christ's behalf, be reconciled to God." The God who reconciled us to Himself has given us the responsibility and ministry of reconciliation. Those who have experienced the reality of personal trespasses that have been forgiven by God in Christ are now ambassadors for Christ. The mission and message of the ambassador is to represent (1) God pleading through us and (2) the plea must be clear – be reconciled to God.

The concern for both forgiveness and reconciliation should be thought of in the active tense. People need to be forgiven and reconciled. There is uneasiness and a form of anxiety if there is no sense of being forgiven by another. The sense of that type forgiveness would be evidenced in the reality of reconciliation and restoration. An important consideration in terms of forgiveness is in terms of when and how it occurs. If I am the offended person, do I seek out the one who caused the offense and offer that person forgiveness, or should I wait until they come to me and ask to be forgiven? There is a two-pronged

Biblical approach. First, Jesus said in the Sermon on the Mount in Matthew 5:23-24, "Therefore if you bring your gift to the altar, and there remember that your brother has something against you, leave your gift there before the altar, and go your way. First be reconciled to your brother, and then come and offer your gift." Jesus is essentially saying take care of first things first. Take care of offering forgiveness and achieving reconciliation. Second, if you are the offending person and you acted in anger, Paul wrote in Ephesians 4:26, "Be angry, and do not sin, do not let the sun go down on your wrath..." If you reacted to another in anger, it needs to be admitted, confessed, and dealt with promptly (preferably on the same day of the expressed anger). The *World Dictionary* defines anger as, "a feeling of great annoyance or antagonism as a result of some real or supposed grievance, rage or wrath." Physiologically, there is the acceleration of the heart rate and elevation of the blood pressure; the rate of breathing increases to get more oxygen into the body and attention narrows. One must understand that anger is both a spiritual and physical issue. It cannot be overemphasized that wrath must be dealt with quickly (before the setting of the sun). This is part of the privilege of forgiveness and reconciliation.

Some choose to ignore the mission and message and would rather magnify the sin of the sinner/offender. It occurs by the personal approach of holding someone accountable for their past sins. Why does this become the approach and practice? The subtle purpose in this response to another's sin/offense is that it: (1) keeps one below or beneath us; (2) it gives us a sense and feeling of spiritual superiority; (3) it ignores and prevents us from confessing the sin of pride; (4) it prevents the possibility of reconciliation and fellowship in the Body of Christ; (5) it prevents us and the Body of Christ from knowing the joy of helping someone become restored in Christ; (6) it restricts us from helping another from growing in the knowledge and grace of the Lord; and (7) it gives one a sense of superiority and authority that is unmerited and undeserved. This type of behavior and practice chooses to forget the reality stated in I Corinthians 6:9-11, "Do you not know that the unrighteous will not inherit the kingdom of God? Do not be deceived. Neither fornicators, nor idolaters, nor adulterers, nor homosexuals, nor sodomites, nor thieves, nor covetous, nor drunkards, nor revilers, nor extortioners will inherit the kingdom of God. And such were some of you. But you were washed, but you were sanctified, but you were justified in the name of the Lord Jesus and by the Spirit of our God." We would do well to remember that before God we were seen as a sinner/offender. The phrase, "and such were some of you," should awaken us to the fact that the grace and mercy of God has granted us reconciliation. In the same manner, we need to share that message of hope to others, to wit, that they can also be "washed, sanctified, and justified in the name of the Lord Jesus Christ."

Why does one have to respond to others in this manner? Why does it become a personal mission and responsibility? Why does one have to set aside personal opinions or biases regarding others and assume the role of an ambassador for Christ? The answer can be found in Romans 15:5-7, "Now may the God of patience and comfort grant you to be like-minded toward one another, according to Christ Jesus, that you may with one mind and one mouth glorify the God and Father of our Lord Jesus Christ. Therefore receive one another, just as Christ also received us, to the glory of God." Just a question to ponder: If man's chief end is to glorify God and enjoy Him forever, won't that be accomplished through the application of these verses in our relationships with all others? We need to be more aware of the fact that we are living amid the cultural chaos that is accelerating and becoming more encompassing. There are many who will be or who already are casualties within the cultural chaos, and sadly, too few who stand out as conquerors.

Ken Sande continues, "Do you sometimes find yourself breaking (or tempted to break) one or more of the Four Promises of Forgiveness sometime after you make them? That's a very normal experience – and believe it or not, it's an invitation from God to draw closer to Him. The key is remembering and applying Hebrews 9:22. That verse tells us that in the universe there is only one source of durable forgiveness: the Cross of Christ. "Without the shedding of blood," the verse says, "there is no forgiveness." For a time, we may be able to forgive someone out of our own willpower or our human desire for reconciliation, but eventually even our best efforts will buckle (yes, even when they are buoyed up by Four Promises). If we want our forgiveness of others to "stick", we ourselves must "stick" continually – to the Cross. So when you sense a long-buried hatchet rising to the surface, don't dwell on those thoughts. Instead, dwell on Christ's forgiveness of your own sin. The more real that becomes for you, the less temptation toward unforgiveness will be."

The one who is active in the attempt to cause us to ignore the mission and message of reconciliation is the adversary (enemy), the devil. We should remember the words of I Peter 5:8-9, "Be sober, be vigilant; because your adversary (enemy) the devil walks about like a roaring lion, seeking whom he may devour. Resist him, steadfast in the faith." One needs to guard against allowing any opportunity for the adversary (enemy) to infiltrate one's life and hinder the mission and message given by Jesus Christ. The One by Whom we have been reconciled expects us to accomplish the task of the ambassador by making known that reconciliation to God is a constant and viable possibility. The reconciliation will bring about an inner peace that surpasses one's ability to understand it. It will affirm within one the declaration of Romans 5:1, "Therefore, having been justified by faith, we have peace with God through our Lord Jesus Christ, through whom also we have access by faith into this grace in which we stand, and rejoice in hope of the glory of God." Alienation departs and being reconciled enters. Why would any ambassador refuse to accept that mission and to declare that message – reconciliation can be one's reality? The serpent will do whatever he can to hinder that mission from going forward and that message being declared. One needs to understand that the serpent is a vanquished foe and the One in us has already gained the victory for us over death, sin and the world. As you go forward on your mission and with the message of reconciliation, keep in mind the words of I John 4:4, "You are of God, little children, and have overcome them, because He who is in you is greater than he who is in the world."

Another part of the revealed character and activity of the serpent is that he is called a deceiver and is skillful in his efforts and methods to deceive. This is a reason why Jesus Christ wanted all to know the precise basis upon which the serpent operates, namely, to deceive by any and all means possible. In John 8:43-44, the Lord Jesus Christ challenges the tactics of the Scribes and Pharisees: "Why do you not understand My speech? Because you are not able to listen to My word. You are of your father the devil, and the desires of your father you want to do. He was a murderer from the beginning, and does not stand in the truth, because there is no truth in him. When he speaks a lie, he speaks from his own resources, for he is a liar and the father of it." Jesus Christ is clear and precise in what He has stated and revealed. There is a crafty and wily enemy who is constant in his pursuit for the mind and soul of mankind. He is relentless and tireless in his desire and effort. He will seek to penetrate one's thinking and desires to achieve his obvious diabolic goals. When Paul refers to this relentlessness of the serpent, he instructs the believers in Ephesus, as well as in all the churches, "we do not wrestle against flesh and blood, but against principalities, against powers, against the rulers of the darkness of this age, against spiritual hosts of wickedness in the heavenly places...above all, take the shield of faith with which you will be able to quench all the fiery darts of the wicked one" (Ephesians 6:12, 16). Paul is indicating that there is a spiritual conflict and one must be aware of it. One must be knowledgeable regarding the tactics employed by the enemy, and equipped to ward off all attempts by the serpent and his minions.

Can one be confident that the spiritual armament will be effective? Is there a sense that this tactic and effort will accomplish the desired goal? What is the determined end for the serpent? In I Corinthians 15:55-58 (ESV), the Apostle Paul makes a bold declaration based upon the resurrection of Jesus Christ. He states, "Death is swallowed up in victory. O death, where is your victory? O death, where is your sting? The sting of death is sin, and the power of sin is the law. But thanks be to God, who gives us the victory through our Lord Jesus Christ. Therefore, my beloved brothers, be steadfast, immovable, always abounding in the work of the Lord, knowing that in the Lord your labor is not in vain." These words are intended to spur on the Christian community in all generations because Christ has conquered sin and death on the believer's behalf. Additionally, there is the assurance of the final victory over the serpent given in Romans 16:20 (ESV), "The God of peace will soon crush Satan under your feet. The grace of our Lord Jesus Christ be with you." The crushing of Satan is consistent with the *protoevangelium* (Latin: first Gospel) given in Genesis 3:14-15 (NIV), "So the Lord God said to the serpent, because you have done this, Cursed are you above all the livestock and all the wild animals! You will crawl on your belly and you will eat dust all the days of your life. And I will put enmity between you and the woman, and between your offspring and hers; he will crush your head, and you will strike his heel." The conflict will be intensive and extensive. Some of the consequences of sin are given in Genesis 3. The hope is that at a given moment and in accordance with God's purpose, the serpent's head will be crushed by the seed of the woman, namely, Jesus Christ. There is an additional indication of the serpent's plight and destiny given in Revelation 20:1-3 (ESV), "Then I saw an angel coming down from heaven, holding in his hand the key to the bottomless pit and a great chain. And he seized the dragon, that ancient serpent, who is the devil and Satan, and bound him…and threw him into the pit, and shut it and sealed it over him, so that he might not deceive the nations any longer…"

    This is the mission and message of the ambassador of Jesus Christ. There is redemption, forgiveness and restoration to fellowship with God in and through the Lord Jesus Christ. He paid the penalty for one's sin in His death on the cross. He secured one's victory over death and the grave in His resurrection from the dead. In Christ alone, one can find and have redemption. In Christ alone, one can find forgiveness for all sins and trespasses. In Christ alone, one can realize the scope and benefit of the grace of God. In Christ alone, one can find and know the reality of fellowship with the Lord.

FOR THOUGHT AND REFLECTION:

If you had to explain "Redemption" to a child, what is the most simple and basic way to do it? What would you utilize to define "redemption"?

When Temptation occurs in your life, in what one of three areas is it most likely to occur? Read I John 2:15-17 as you answer this question!

What context of life can cause you to be most vulnerable in terms Temptation? Read Psalm 1:1-3 as you answer this question!

Who/What is the primary instigator and source of Temptation?

Can he be conquered by you?

What must you do to have the source of Temptation leave you alone and remove himself from your life? Read James 4:6-8 and list some of the minimum behavioral modification that must be occurring in your life!

As you implement these new behaviors, what should you do in terms of the devil (See: Ephesians 4:27)? What will the devil's response and reaction be to your new behaviors?

Trust in the Lord, and do good...
Delight yourself also in the Lord,
And He shall give you the desires of your heart.
Commit your way to the Lord, Trust also in Him,
And He shall bring it to pass.
He shall bring forth your righteousness...
Rest in the Lord, and wait patiently for Him.
Psalm 37:3-7 (Selected)

4. Application of the Let Us to Us

It is abundantly clear that the "Let Us" as it refers to the plans and purposes of the Godhead has an additional application, namely, how the "Let Us" impacts "us". Just as the "Let Us" determined the scope and parameters of The Creation, even so the "Let Us" has a design and purpose for those who are part of the new creation. This is gleaned from II Corinthians 5:15, 17, "...and He died for all, that those who live should live no longer for themselves, but for Him Who died for them and rose again. Therefore, if anyone is in Christ, he is a new creation; old things have passed away; behold, all things have become new." The "Let Us" has the governance over what "old things" should pass away, as well as what "new things" must come to fruition and reality in one's life. It involves a new focus and a new determination in and for one's life. It also involves and entails a work of God's Grace that is known as Sanctification and/or the development of spiritual maturity. Basically, it is defined in the Westminster Shorter Catechism 35 as, "...the work of God's free grace, whereby we are renewed in the whole man after the image of God, and are enabled more and more to die unto sin, and live unto righteousness." It is a process begun that will continue throughout one's spiritual life and journey. Paul stated as much when he wrote in Philippians 1:6, "...being confident of this very thing, that He Who has begun a good work in you will complete it until the day of Jesus Christ."

If this generation, living "Amid The Cultural Chaos," is to impact the culture of the day, it will only occur by the presence and power of the "Let Us" functioning within us and through us. If there is a possibility of reaching this generation with an alternative to the secular and entitlement culture and mindset, we need to embrace the "Let Us" in our lives within the church community. We need to grasp that as we live amid the cultural chaos we are on a rescue mission. Our task is to reach out to those who are living as casualties and attempt to bring them to the place where they experience what it means to be a conqueror through the Lord Jesus Christ. Is there risk and danger in this mission? The answer is: Yes! Jude 1:22-23 states the extent to which one must go during the rescue mission: "And on some have compassion, making a distinction; but others save with fear, pulling them out of the fire, hating even the garment defiled by the flesh." Why are we to do this type of rescue? It is to bring others into a purposeful relationship with The Redeemer. In that relationship, there will be an involvement with others of like precious faith. It is also part of our task to implement the "Let Us" factor within the "let us" of the fellowship of believers. The concept of this relationship and indication of the "Let Us" application is found in the "one another" and the "let us" passages in Scripture.

There are many references to the relational obligation of "one another" behavior. Some of the obvious ones are: Love one another; Be kind to one another; Fellowship with one another; Do not slander one another; Offer hospitality to one another;

etc. In like manner, there are several "let us" references. There are fifteen "let us" passages in The Book of Hebrews. We need to keep in mind that "let us" grammatically is a Hortatory Subjunctive (a statement urging others to join in some action). The focus of this Chapter is Hebrews 10:24, "...let us consider one another...to stir up love and good works..." Too often, the "let us" obligations are glossed over and are viewed as an ideal but not an enjoinder for a personal application. It is vital for the "let us" passages to be applied as a call to action that is bold, courageous and significant. It includes the enlisting of others to participate in this noble effort and journey. When "let us" appears in a text, it is inclusive and all are to enthusiastically become involved in the task at hand.

In a world that is marked by conflict, unrest and chaos, as well as devastating storms and ensuing turmoil, it is right to be reminded that the "Let Us" Who created the world and everything/everyone in it, has a plan and purpose for His world and our lives. In a culture that is seemingly obsessed with the secular lifestyle and entitlement mindset, the "Let Us" has been steadily obscured. However, the "Let Us" Who created and controls all things, has a purpose for the "let us" of His new creation. Hebrews 10:24 instructs one to have a particular focus, "And let us consider one another in order to stir up love and good works," The words are succinct. (1) The Principle is: "Let us..." (2) The Purpose is, "...consider one another..." (3) The Performance is, "...to stir up love and good deeds..." One way this can be measured is in terms of how one responds to disasters and human needs. One can shrug off any interest or concern by rationalizing that "this too shall pass" or "they'll be alright and manage." Additionally, the United States federal government has established FEMA (Federal Emergency Management Agency) that has many more resources to assist those most in need. Another way people choose to respond is to look to the Salvation Army, Samaritans Purse, World Vision, or the Red Cross to provide services and supplies during a disaster. We must never forget that one needs to guard against indifference to human suffering and/or being dispassionate toward those with need.

A meaningful expression of the "let us" principle appears in a Fall 2012 Thanksgiving response letter of The Jimmie Hale Mission located in Birmingham, Alabama. Part of the letter is a Purpose Statement of the Mission: "The Mission has been a rest stop for the tired; a feeding station for the hungry; a sanctuary for the troubled; a stepping stone for the struggling; and a spiritual hospital for the hurting." A part of the signature to the letter is Proverbs 19:17 (NASB), "He who is gracious to the poor man lends to the Lord, and He will repay him for his good deed." The potential reward should not be the occasion or motive for a gift to the needy, but rather the individual's response from a compassionate and grateful heart. It is good to remember the phrase, "There, but for the grace of God, go I." It carries with it the idea that, "I too, like someone seen to have suffered misfortune, might have suffered a similar fate, but for God's mercy, love and grace."

A tension in maintaining a sense of mission can arise when one allows self-interests and self-preservation to become an all-consuming concern. On the broader scale, is there a sense of the needs of others in the world? The answer is usually affirmative. With a narrower focus, does one have a sense of personal needs, wants and desires that should be cared for first? The answer is usually and emphatically affirmative. Obviously, there needs to be a balance in this area. The subtle part of the tension is in terms of (a) what constitutes selflessness versus (b) what constitutes selfishness. If one was to weigh on a balance scale (a) the needs of others and a personal response to those needs, and (b) the personal needs of self and family, would the scale be evenly balanced or would it be tipped more toward the needs of others or more to one's personal needs?

James 2:14-20 (The Message) sets before us a balance and mandate in terms of faith and action. "Dear friends, do you think you'll get anywhere in this if you learn all the right words but never do anything? Does merely talking about faith indicate that a person really has it? For instance, you come upon an old friend dressed in rags and half-starved and say, Good morning, friend! Be clothed in Christ! Be filled with the Holy Spirit! Then you walk off without providing so much as a coat or a cup of soup - where does that get you? Isn't it obvious that God-talk without God-acts is outrageous nonsense? I can already hear one of you agreeing by saying, sounds good. You take care of the faith department. I'll handle the works department. Not so fast. You can no more show me your works apart from your faith than

I can show you my faith apart from my works. Faith and works, works and faith, fit together hand in glove. Do I hear you professing to believe in the one and only God, but then observe you complacently sitting back as if you had done something wonderful? That's just great. Demons do that, but what good does it do them? Use your heads! Do you suppose for a minute that you can cut faith and works in two and not end up with a corpse on your hands?" The point is that a follower of Christ must live out the Christian profession and commitment in a both/and manner rather than in an either/or choice. Be reminded of what Jesus declared in the scene where He is separating the sheep from the goats, Matthew 25:31-40 (NIV), "When the Son of Man comes in his glory, and all the angels with him, he will sit on his throne in heavenly glory. All the nations will be gathered before him, and He will separate the people one from another as a shepherd separates the sheep from the goats. He will put the sheep on his right and the goats on His left. Then the King will say to those on his right, Come, you who are blessed by My Father; take your inheritance, the kingdom prepared for you since the creation of the world. For I was hungry and you gave me something to eat, I was thirsty and you gave me something to drink, I was a stranger and you invited me in, I needed clothes and you clothed me, I was sick and you looked after me, I was in prison and you came to visit me. Then the righteous will answer him, Lord, when did we see You hungry and feed You, or thirsty and give You something to drink? When did we see You a stranger and invite You in, or needing clothes and clothe You? When did we see You sick or in prison and go to visit You? The King will reply, I tell you the truth, whatever you did for one of the least of these brothers of mine, you did for Me."

The lesson to be learned is that one must look at people in the world, especially those who are needy, through the eyes of Jesus Christ. There should never be an ulterior motive for sharing and caring for the hungry, the thirsty, the stranger needing shelter, the ones needing adequate clothing, the sick who need care, the imprisoned who should be visited. The response to others in their predicament should be normal and natural. Are there some who will endeavor to work benevolence for their own selfish interests? Yes! Are there those who will abuse another's generosity and connive to take advantage of it? Yes! Are there those who feign helplessness and who are motivated by their personal selfishness? Yes! Will some waste and squander that which they have been given? Yes!

The fact that some will abuse another's generosity should neither cause any cynicism regarding one's providing for others, nor a suspicion that those seeking help don't really need as much as they are seeking. It is always best to provide with a genuine and sincere desire/effort to care for and help others. A fond memory is a time when a stranger came to the door of our home (a Church Manse adjacent to the Church Building) and asked for something to eat. We were nearing the completion of our evening meal and invited the stranger in to sit at our table with us. He ate one plateful of food and asked if he could have another. After consuming the second plateful, he was grateful and thanked us. When he left our home, he asked if I could take him to the highway so he could continue to hitch-hike. Later on, our young children said, "Now that man was really hungry." We don't know who this man was or where he had come from, nor did we know where he was going. I spoke with him about the Lord and gave him a New Testament. I asked him to read it and he said that he would do so. We can only hope that he did so and desired to be in a redemptive relationship with the Lord Jesus Christ. No one can ever anticipate or calculate how a person will respond to one's best effort to meet a need. There was another occasion when a man came to the door of our home and asked for something to eat. Our meal consisted of Bologna Sandwiches. He was offered what we were eating and he emphatically refused. He handed it back and said to my wife, "I wanted steak and potatoes – eat that sandwich yourself." My wife responded that she would inasmuch as that was our evening meal. He went away having neglected a genuine effort to include him in the food that was available at the moment. We have no idea what his plight in life was or what happened to him. He walked away expressing disappointment that he was not treated differently and offered something more lavish.

    The principle of mission and message is that it is motivated by compassion and actuated with kindness. On December 24, 1914, a sermon by Charles H. Spurgeon on Matthew 9:36-38 was circulated. The text read: "But when He saw the multitudes, He was moved with compassion for them, because they were weary and scattered, like sheep having no shepherd. Then He said to His disciples, the harvest truly is plentiful, but the laborers are few. Therefore pray the Lord of the harvest to send out laborers into His harvest." He was focused primarily on verse 36, "...He was moved with compassion for them, because they were weary and scattered, like sheep having no shepherd." Regarding the compassion of Jesus Christ, Spurgeon noted: "This is said of Christ Jesus several times in the New Testament. The original word is a very remarkable one. It is not found in classic Greek. It is not found in the Septuagint. The fact is, it was a word coined by the evangelists themselves. They did not find one in the whole Greek language that suited their purpose, and therefore they had to make one. It is expressive of the deepest emotion; a striving of the bowels—a yearning of the innermost nature with pity...I suppose that when our Savior looked upon certain sights, those who watched him closely perceived that his internal agitation was very great, his emotions were very deep, and then his face betrayed it, his eyes gushed like founts with tears, and you saw that his big heart was ready to burst with pity for the sorrow upon which his eyes were gazing. He was moved with compassion. His whole nature was agitated with commiseration for the sufferers before him."

One can only wonder whether or not a level of compassion is observable with those who are designated as the ambassadors of Jesus Christ. The mission and message should reflect intensity and urgency as the mission is undertaken and the message is proclaimed. Spurgeon continued his commentary with remarks on, "Some Of The Foresights Of His Compassion."

Some of the foresights offered are: "The Lord has gone from us, but as he knew what would happen while he was away, he has, with blessed forethought, provided for our wants. Well he knew that we should never be able to preserve the truth pure by tradition. That is a stream that always muddies and defiles everything. So in tender forethought he has given us the consolidated testimony, the unchangeable truth in his own Book; for he was moved with compassion. He knew the priests would not preach the gospel; he knew that no order of men could be trusted to hold fast sound doctrine from generation to generation; he knew there would be hirelings that dare not be faithful to their conscience lest they should lose their pay; while there would be others who love to tickle men's ears and flatter their vanity rather than to tell out plainly and distinctly the whole counsel of God. Therefore, he has put it here, so that if you live where there is no preacher of the gospel, you have the old Book to go to. He is moved with compassion for you. For where a man cannot go, the Book can go, and where in silence no voice is heard, the still clear voice of this blessed Book can reach the heart. Because he knew the people would require this sacred teaching, and could not have it otherwise, he was moved with compassion towards us all, and gave us the blessed Book of inspired God-breathed Scripture."

As one looks at the state of the "church" and the "Christian community" one-hundred years after Spurgeon's sermon was circulated, one can sense the prophetic tone of his comments. One can readily observe that (1) tradition muddies the water of the day; (2) those in organized religion do not preach the gospel; (3) adherence to sound doctrine is being sacrificed; (4) there is a class of hirelings who view ministry as a job and do not preach with conviction lest they lose their pay; and (5) those who are ego-driven and who thrive on the praise of men rather than telling plainly and distinctly the whole counsel of God. The professional clergy has drifted far from a level of commitment similar to that of the Apostle Paul in Acts 20:22-24, "And see, now I go bound in the spirit to Jerusalem, not knowing the things that will happen to me there, except that the Holy Spirit testifies in every city, saying that chains and tribulations await me. But none of these things move me; nor do I count my life dear to myself, so that I may finish my race with joy, and the ministry which I received from the Lord Jesus, to testify to the gospel of the grace of God." Paul had a singular focus, namely, "...the ministry which I received from the Lord Jesus, to testify to the gospel of the grace of God." One can only hope and pray that God will call a new generation of men, who with conviction and commitment, carry out His mission and proclaim His message to this generation that has ignored Him and His Word.

Spurgeon concluded his commentary on the compassion of Jesus Christ with these words: "He is never happier than when he is relieving and retrieving the forlorn, the abject, and the outcast. He despises not any that confess their sins and seek his mercy. No pride nestles in his dear heart, no sarcastic word rolls off his gracious tongue, no bitter expression falls from his blessed lips. He still receives the guilty. Pray to him now. Now let the silent prayer go up, My Savior, have pity upon me; be moved with compassion towards me, for if misery be any qualification for mercy, I am a fit object for thy compassion. Oh! save me for thy mercy's sake! Amen."

In the midst of a nation of despair, and one that had forsaken the Lord, Jeremiah reminds himself of Who the Lord is and that which is a personification of His character. In like manner, as we live "Amid The Cultural Chaos" of our day, we can identify with his sentiment and commitment. Jeremiah writes about this in Lamentations 3:21-32 (selected) "This I recall to my mind, therefore I have hope. Through the Lord's mercies we are not consumed, because His compassions fail not. They are new every morning; great is Your faithfulness. The Lord is my portion, says my soul, therefore I hope in Him! The Lord is good to those who wait for Him, to the soul who seeks Him. It is good that one should hope and wait quietly for the salvation of the Lord…For the Lord will not cast off forever. Though He causes grief, yet He will show compassion according to the multitude of His mercies."

The devotional thoughts shared by Dr. A. W. Tozer, even though they were written more than fifty years ago, are very timely for us to consider. In a paragraph titled, "Failure and Success: The School of Failure", he writes his thoughts based upon Psalm 103:13-14, "As a father pities his children, so the Lord pities those who fear Him. For He knows our frame; He remembers that we are dust." He then shared: "…Brother Lawrence expressed the highest moral wisdom when he testified that if he stumbled and fell he turned at once to God and said, 'O Lord, this is what You may expect of me if You leave me to myself.' He then accepted forgiveness, thanked God and gave himself no further concern about the matter. In "The Warfare of the Spirit," Dr. Tozer then added a personal prayer: "Oh Lord, some of us have graduate degrees from this school (of failure)! Help us to learn well from our failures, to accept Christ's forgiveness, and to move on. Give victory for today, I pray, in Jesus' name. Amen."

Edward Kennedy stated these words as part of the eulogy for his assassinated brother, Robert F. Kennedy: "...It is a revolutionary world we live in, and this generation at home and around the world has had thrust upon it a greater burden of responsibility than any generation that has ever lived. Some believe there is nothing one man or one woman can do against the enormous array of the world's ills. Yet many of the world's great movements, of thought and action, have flowed from the work of a single individual. A young monk began the Protestant reformation; a young general extended an empire from Macedonia to the borders of the earth; a young woman reclaimed the territory of France; and it was a young Italian explorer who discovered the New World, and the 32 year-old Thomas Jefferson who [pro]claimed that "all men are created equal." These men moved the world, and so can we all. Few will have the greatness to bend history itself, but each of us can work to change a small portion of events, and in the total of all those acts will be written the history of this generation. It is from numberless diverse acts of courage and belief that human history is shaped. Each time a man stands up for an ideal, or acts to improve the lot of others, or strikes out against injustice, he sends forth a tiny ripple of hope, and crossing each other from a million different centers of energy and daring, those ripples build a current that can sweep down the mightiest walls of oppression and resistance. Few are willing to brave the disapproval of their fellows, the censure of their colleagues, the wrath of their society. Moral courage is a rarer commodity than bravery in battle or great intelligence. Yet it is the one essential, vital quality for those who seek to change a world that yields most painfully to change. And I believe that in this generation those with the courage to enter the moral conflict will find themselves with companions in every corner of the globe...For the fortunate among us, there is the temptation to follow the easy and familiar paths of personal ambition and financial success so grandly spread before those who enjoy the privilege of education. But that is not the road history has marked out for us. Like it or not, we live in times of danger and uncertainty. But they are also more open to the creative energy of men than any other time in history. All of us will ultimately be judged, and as the years pass we will surely judge ourselves on the effort we have contributed to building a new world society and the extent to which our ideals and goals have shaped that event. The future does not belong to those who are content with today, apathetic toward common problems and their fellow man alike, timid and fearful in the face of new ideas and bold projects. Rather it will belong to those who can blend vision, reason and courage in a personal commitment to the ideals and great enterprises of American Society. Our future may lie beyond our vision, but it is not completely beyond our control. It is the shaping impulse of America that neither fate nor nature nor the irresistible tides of history, but the work of our own hands, matched to reason and principle, that will determine our destiny. There is pride in that, even arrogance, but there is also experience and truth. In any event, it is the only way we can live. That is the way he lived. That is what he leaves us. My brother need not be idealized, or enlarged in death beyond what he was in life; to be remembered simply as a good and decent man, who saw wrong and tried to right it, saw suffering and tried to heal it, saw war and tried to stop it. Those of us who loved him and who take him to his rest today, pray that what he was to us and what he wished for others will someday come to pass for all the world. As he said many times, in many parts of this nation, to those he touched and who sought to touch him: 'Some men see things as they are and say why. I dream things that never were and say why not.'"

If this could be said of one in the secular and political arena, should it not challenge each of us to aspire similar and higher goals within the spiritual context? If this was being said about one whose behavior was at variance with Biblical standards and virtues, should it not cause the follower of Christ to greater care and higher regard for God's standards and requirements for His people? If we are being defined by Jesus Christ according to His words in Matthew 25:36-40, will He define you/us as behaving like the goats or like the sheep?

FOR THOUGHT AND REFLECTION:

In terms of the "new creation" lifestyle, what are some of the "old things" that must pass away?
What are some of the "new things" that should occur as the transformation from old to new takes place?

What three things are absolutely essential for the new creature in Christ? Read Ephesians 4:22-24 and Colossians 3:8-10 to assist you with this answer.

If you used a scale of one to ten, how would you score yourself in terms of the progress you are achieving in this transformational process?

Consider Ephesians 4:30-32. If one fails to implement the "new things" in his/her life, and neglects the outward display of human compassion, what is the result of this negative behavior? What do you believe the consequence would be for the one who violates and/or ignores these verses?

What is your personal level of "compassion"? Do you respond willingly and enthusiastically to meet the needs of others?

Is Matthew 25:34-40 applicable to you and a reflection of how Jesus sees you responding "Amid The Cultural Chaos?" What does Jesus Christ require of you in order that you will be identified as a sheep rather than as a goat? Is there a valid exception or an acceptable excuse that grants one latitude in terms of the directives of Jesus Christ?

Whatever you do, work at it with all your heart, as working for the Lord, not for men, since you know that you will receive an inheritance from the Lord as a reward.

It is the Lord Christ you are serving.

Colossians 3:23-24 (NIV)

5. The Church - Form and Function

The idea of "Form and Function" is utilized in many fields of study. An Architect looks at forms and functions and may ask: will an ornate form of a building facilitate the function for which it is being erected? Sometimes, in addition to form and function, the term "fit" is included. The idea of function is commonplace today. Dials on an appliance give one a choice of Function – bake, broil, toast or convection. Family Counselors look at a household in terms of it being functional or dysfunctional. Children with behavioral issues are viewed as being normal (functioning properly) or abnormal (dysfunctional and needing assistance for behavior modification). Many times, it means use of medications (Ritalin or Prozac, or both) to bring about the modification of a defined behavior. In the field and world of electronics, one must understand the function of the device one is attempting to use. This idea of form and function also filters into the church in terms of how and where it meets; the type service it conducts - contemporary or formal; the music that is used - classical, modern, or gospel; the wardrobe of worship leaders - clerical robes, business suits, or slacks and open-collar shirts; etc. Somewhere along the way, the Church has made a decision that it must change in order to be relative in and to a changing world. This decision should include that as it functions amid the cultural chaos there is a duty and mission to reflect the ministry of Jesus Christ. This would entail the task of the Church to seek the lost in order that they might be saved. It is the idea of rescuing the casualties of the culture so that they might find deliverance and new life in The One in Whom one can be more than a conqueror.

The Church should have a focus, vision, mission and purpose. It should stand as the only reasonable alternative to atheism and secularism. It should stand astride the gulf between secularism on the one hand and spirituality on the other. In effect, the Church of Jesus Christ should be at the crossroad of life where people make eternal choices and decisions. The Church should direct all men to the cross which is the only means by which one may bridge the vast gulf that separates the secular world from the heavenly kingdom. The question is: Is the Church today "A Cultural Reality" or "A Cultural Casualty?" Does the Church reflect the True Light or has it succumbed to the influences of haziness and darkness? Is the Church a viable part of the solution or a contributor to the cultural problem? When the Church officiates at same-gender marriages and ordains those who embrace an alternative lifestyle, is it representing and projecting the unequivocal message of God's Word? At this point, has the culture impacted the "church" rather than the Church having impacted the culture? The message of the Word of God hasn't changed but the message emanating from the church has diminished. In many places, the "church" has become all things to all men but not to the end that salvation and redeeming grace will be affected in the lives of those who have minimized God and His Standards. The Church needs to be less accommodating to the world's standards and dictates and more assertive in terms of God's standards and dictates.

In an Essay presented by J. Gresham Machen in 1933, he set the tone and established the parameters for The Church in his remarks on: "The Responsibility Of The Church In Our New Age." He said: "The responsibility of the church in the new age is the same as its responsibility in every age. It is to testify that this world is lost in sin; that the span of human life—no, all the length of human history—is an infinitesimal island in the awful depths of eternity; that there is a mysterious, holy, living God, Creator of all, Upholder of all, infinitely beyond all; that he has revealed himself to us in his Word and offered us communion with himself through Jesus Christ the Lord; that there is no other salvation, for individuals or for nations, save this, but that this salvation is full and free, and that whoever possesses it has for himself and for all others to whom he may be the instrument of bringing it a treasure compared with which all the kingdoms of the earth—no, all the wonders of the starry heavens—are as the dust of the street. An unpopular message it is—an impractical message, we are told. But it is the message of the Christian church. Neglect it, and you will have destruction; heed it, and you will have life."

It echoes and affirms the message of the apostles Peter and John in Acts 4:10-13, "...let it be known to you all, and to all the people of Israel, that by the name of Jesus Christ of Nazareth, whom you crucified, whom God raised from the dead, by Him this man stands here before you whole. This is the stone which was rejected by you builders, which has become the chief cornerstone. Nor is there salvation in any other, for there is no other name under heaven given among men by which we must be saved. Now when they saw the boldness of Peter and John, and perceived that they were uneducated and untrained men, they marveled. And they realized that they had been with Jesus." They stated the truth about Jesus Christ unequivocally and distanced from any degree of vagueness. The Church has come a long way from its more primitive form in the first century. The men were ordinary; some were uneducated and untrained, taught only as disciples who travelled with Jesus. The places where they purposed to worship God and study His Word varied. Sometimes they were able to approach the Temple, but usually they met in homes, or fields or wherever people would gather. The Church today is less primitive. The clergy are professionally educated. In some Church groups, men are required to have an undergraduate degree in some major field of study, as well as graduate studies in an approved Seminary. A gnawing question is - at the end of the day, can it be said by the watching world of the twenty-first century clergy - "they realized that they had been with Jesus"?

Is there a minimum requirement and standard for a normal Christian Life? What determines whether or not a spiritual behavior is normal, practical, functional and Biblical? There is no itemized list that can enumerate the requirement for the normal and functional Christian Life. One of the starting points is Romans 8:1-17. This passage teaches the role and impact of the

Holy Spirit within the life and lifestyle of the normal and functional Christian. The statement of fact that is relevant is given in verse 1: "There is therefore now no condemnation to those who are in Christ Jesus, who do not walk according to the flesh, but according to the Spirit." It addresses: (1) A Spiritual Relationship, namely, being in Christ Jesus and no longer subjected to condemnation; and (2) A Spiritual Commitment, namely, being under the control of the Holy Spirit so that one no longer walks according to the flesh but has been transformed and now walks according to the Spirit. Every part and aspect of ones life must be lived under the control and authority of the Holy Spirit. It is necessary for one to know and live the godly life consistently. This will require a fixed focus on Jesus Christ and the Word of God. It will also require complete guidance and control by the Holy Spirit. The phrase, "walk by the Spirit," occurs in Galatians 5:16 and 5:25. The sense being conveyed is that one has to learn to walk by the enablement of the Spirit. The demands of the consecrated and holy life are too great for one to attempt to meet those demands apart from the Spirit's control. The Spirit will enable the walk of the believer in the same manner in which he enables a believer's prayer (Romans 8:26-27) to be presented at the throne of God in full and complete accordance with the will of God.

What are some of the characteristics, qualities, mannerisms and habits we should know and practice as one walks by the Spirit's enablement? In Romans 8:4, we are to be known as one who is "walking according to the Spirit." Paul teaches the importance of this truth in Galatians 5:16-17, "Walk in the Spirit, and you shall not fulfill the lust of the flesh. For the flesh lusts against the Spirit, and the Spirit against the flesh; and these are contrary to one another, so that you do not do the things that you wish." An additional instruction is given in Galatians 5:24-25 (The Message): "Among those who belong to Christ, everything connected with getting our own way and mindlessly responding to what everyone else calls necessities is killed off for good - crucified. Since this is the kind of life we have chosen, the life of the Spirit, let us make sure that we do not just hold it as an idea in our heads or a sentiment in our hearts, but work out its implications in every detail of our lives."

Why is this point made and stressed? Romans 5:5-8 explains: "For those who live according to the flesh set their minds on the things of the flesh, but those who live according to the Spirit, the things of the Spirit. For to be carnally minded is death, but to be spiritually minded is life and peace, because the carnal mind is enmity against God; for it is not subject to the law of God, nor indeed can be. So then, those who are in the flesh cannot please God." The Message states these verses: "Those who think they can do it on their own end up obsessed with measuring their own moral muscle but never get around to exercising it in real life. Those who trust God's action in them find that God's Spirit is in them - living and breathing God! Obsession with self in these matters is a dead end; attention to God leads us out into the open, into a spacious, free life. Focusing on the self is the opposite of focusing on God. Anyone completely absorbed in self ignores God, ends up thinking more about self than God. That person ignores who God is and what he is doing. God isn't pleased when people choose to ignore Him and His guidance for them."

Paul hastens to state ones relationship and position, in Romans 8:9-11, "But you are not in the flesh but in the Spirit, if indeed the Spirit of God dwells in you. Now if anyone does not have the Spirit of Christ, he is not His. And if Christ is in you, the body is dead because of sin, but the Spirit is life because of righteousness. But if the Spirit of Him who raised Jesus from the dead dwells in you, He who raised Christ from the dead will also give life to your mortal bodies through His Spirit who dwells in you." These are magnificent words (a) "if Christ is in you", and (b) "if the Spirit...dwells in you." The Godhead is actively involved within one to conform one to the image of Christ and to prepare one for entrance into God's heavenly kingdom. This truth should never be taken for granted or in a theoretical way. It is necessary for the validation and verification to be factual as the transforming process occurs. The fact of Christ in you and the Spirit dwelling in you must be observable, not by what one says, but by what one's life reveals. The essence of this lifestyle is expressed in II Corinthians 3:1-4, when Paul wrote, "Do we begin again to commend ourselves? Or do we need, as some others, epistles of commendation to you or letters of commendation from you? You are our epistle written in our hearts, known and read by all men; clearly you are an epistle of Christ, ministered by us, written not with ink but by the Spirit of the living God, not on tablets of stone but on tablets of flesh, that is, of the heart." The picture is one of the Spirit of the Living God inscribing in one's heart all that is a priority for the godly life and lifestyle. It's not external, standards and functions chiseled in stone, but internal, where the Holy Spirit is persuading, instructing and guiding one into all of God's truth. It is the function and ministry of the Holy Spirit disclosed by Jesus in John 16:7-11, "Nevertheless I tell you the truth. It is to your advantage that I go away; for if I do not go away, the Helper will not come to you; but if I depart, I will send Him to you. And when He has come, He will convict the world of sin, and of righteousness, and of judgment: of sin, because they do not believe in Me; of righteousness, because I go to My Father and you see Me no more; of judgment, because the ruler of this world is judged." Paraphrased in The Message, this passage reads: "So let me say it again, this truth: It's better for you that I leave. If I don't leave, the Friend won't come. But if I go, I'll send him to you. When he comes, he'll expose the error of the godless world's view of sin, righteousness, and judgment: He'll show them that their refusal to believe in Me is their basic sin; that righteousness comes from above, where I am with the Father, out of their sight and control; that judgment takes place as the ruler of this godless world is brought to trial and convicted." Part of what the indwelling Spirit is inscribing upon one's heart is "...that righteousness comes from above, where I am with the Father, out of their sight and control..."

Understanding and appreciating a life and function guided and controlled by the Spirit of the Living God should grant one a sense of freedom and greater commitment. There will be a clearer understanding and application of Romans 8:12-13, "Therefore, brethren, we are debtors--not to the flesh, to live according to the flesh. For if you live according to the flesh you will die; but if by the Spirit you put to death the deeds of the body, you will live." A key phrase is to "put to death the deeds of the body." It's not a personal effort of merely suppressing the cravings and desires of the flesh by ones own ability or self-discipline. It will include that only as it is being energized and controlled by the Indwelling Spirit of the Living God. The action that is occurring is the process whereby the Holy Spirit enables one to die more and more unto sin and to live more and more unto Christ. This is known in the Scriptures as sanctification and perfection. The concern of the writer of Hebrews was for the believer to grow in grace and to move on toward completion in Christ. In Hebrews 6:1, it is expressed: "Therefore, leaving the discussion of the elementary principles of Christ, let us go on to perfection, not laying again the foundation of repentance from dead works and of faith toward God..." The fact is that Christ is in you. The additional fact is that the Holy Spirit is dwelling in you. The focus is for the Holy Spirit to do His work that will result in sanctification in one's life. This should not allow the believer to conclude that such a renewal and transformation will occur passively. The believer is to be active in terms of the choices one makes and the places one willingly goes. There is a spiritual discipline that one must desire and develop as one walks by the enablement of the Spirit.

The *Westminster Larger Catechism* asks and answers: "What is sanctification? Sanctification is a work of God's grace, whereby they whom God has, before the foundation of the world, chosen to be holy, are in time, through the powerful operation of his Spirit applying the death and resurrection of Christ unto them, renewed in their whole man after the image of God; having the seeds of repentance unto life, and all other saving graces, put into their hearts, and those graces so stirred up, increased, and strengthened, as that they more and more die unto sin, and rise unto newness of life."

How does one know if this work of the Holy Spirit is actually occurring within one? Paul states in Romans 8:14-17, "For as many as are led by the Spirit of God, these are sons of God. For you did not receive the spirit of bondage again to fear, but you received the Spirit of adoption by whom we cry out, Abba, Father. The Spirit Himself bears witness with our spirit that we are children of God, and if children, then heirs--heirs of God and joint heirs with Christ, if indeed we suffer with Him, that we may also be glorified together." The particulars of the relationship that brings newness of life is marked by certain realities: (1) being led by the Spirit of God; (2) being aware that one has been adopted into the body of Christ; (3) an intimacy with the Heavenly Father to Whom one may cry out, Abba, Father; (4) the reassurance as the Spirit bears witness with our spirit affirming that we are the children of God; (5) learning that this new relationship in Christ causes one to be an heir and joint heir with Jesus Christ – but – (6) vital to this new life – "if indeed we suffer with Him, that we may also be glorified together." It is described in Hebrews 13:12-14, "Therefore Jesus also, that He might sanctify the people with His own blood, suffered outside the gate. Therefore let us go forth to Him, outside the camp, bearing His reproach. For here we have no continuing city, but we seek the one to come."

What is the thrust of "...suffer with Him, that we may also be glorified together...?" As we think of Form and Function within the context of the existent chaotic culture, what meaning does "suffer with Him" mean for us? In II Timothy 2:11-14, we get a glimpse of the meaning: "This is a faithful saying: For if we died with Him, We shall also live with Him. If we endure, we shall also reign with Him. If we deny Him, He also will deny us. If we are faithless, He remains faithful; He cannot deny Himself. Remind them of these things, charging them before the Lord not to strive about words to no profit, to the ruin of the hearers." The idea of "endure" is indicative of the pressures that a chaotic culture may inflict upon one who is faithful to God and His standards. No one should be surprised because of opposition to the Gospel and those who both embrace and proclaim it. Peter offered a reminder to the persecuted church of his day when he stated, I Peter 3:12-18, "For the eyes of the Lord are on the righteous, and His ears are open to their prayers; but the face of the Lord is against those who do evil. And who is he who will harm you if you become followers of what is good? But even if you should suffer for righteousness(') sake, you are blessed. And do not be afraid of their threats, nor be troubled. But sanctify the Lord God in your hearts, and always be ready to give a defense to everyone who asks you a reason for the hope that is in you, with meekness and fear; having a good conscience, that when they defame you as evildoers, those who revile your good conduct in Christ may be ashamed. For it is better, if it is the will of God, to suffer for doing good than for doing evil. For Christ also suffered once for sins, the just for the unjust, that He might bring us to God, being put to death in the flesh but made alive by the Spirit." His focus and preparation for the flock of God was: "if you should suffer for righteousness sake, you are blessed." Peter had a clear sense of the times in which he lived and the generation to whom he was to minister. His additional shared concern was: "For it is better, if it is the will of God, to suffer for doing good than for doing evil."

The cultural issues of our day do not emanate from the political or secular sphere. If that was the case, one might be tempted to initiate The Crusades of the twenty-first century. Paul stated it boldly and clearly that one needed to be equipped with the whole armor of God. He also gives the primary reason why this is vital. In Ephesians 6:10-13, he writes: "Finally, my brethren, be strong in the Lord and in the power of His might. Put on the whole armor of God that you may be able to stand against the wiles of the devil. For we do not wrestle against flesh and blood, but against principalities, against powers, against the rulers of the darkness of this age, against spiritual hosts of wickedness in the heavenly places. Therefore take up the whole armor of God that you may be able to withstand in the evil day, and having done all, to stand." Note the reasons for the armor of God protection and defense: (1) stand against the wiles of the devil; (2) we're not in a flesh and blood battle; (3) it is a spiritual battle that entails and involves a defense against a) principalities; b) powers; c) rulers of darkness of this age; d) spiritual hosts of wickedness in the heavenly places. It is a fierce battle and conflict that will necessitate one who will "endure" for Christ's sake. The NLT translates this text: "A final word: Be strong with the Lord's mighty power. Put on all of God's armor so that you will be able to stand firm against all strategies and tricks of the devil. For we are not fighting against people made of flesh and blood, but against the evil rulers and authorities of the unseen world, against those mighty powers of darkness who rule this world, and against wicked spirits in the heavenly realms. Use every piece of God's armor to resist the enemy in the time of evil, so that after the battle you will still be standing firm."

The "church" needs to reexamine where it is and how it became what it is today. Adapting to the cultural pressures was and is a mistake. The Church is supposed to be the herald of the Gospel and representative of the True Light, Jesus Christ. The Church is to be involved in the rescuing of cultural casualties – not becoming a casualty in the process. If Jesus Christ was walking upon the earth today, He might be cleansing many of the buildings that identify themselves as a "church". Far too many "church-types" have allowed for and incorporated that which God neither authorized nor condones. Revelation 2 and 3 is a good study of the "church" and how Jesus Christ views it and what He demands of it. One representative observation by Jesus Christ is Revelation 2:18-24, "And to the angel of the church in Thyatira write, these things says the Son of God, who has eyes like a flame of fire, and His feet like fine brass: I know your works, love, service, faith, and your patience; and as for your works, the last are more than the first. Nevertheless I have a few things against you, because you allow that woman Jezebel, who calls herself a prophetess, to teach and seduce My servants to commit sexual immorality and eat things sacrificed to idols. And I gave her time to repent of her sexual immorality, and she did not repent. Indeed I will cast her into a sickbed, and those who commit adultery with her into great tribulation, unless they repent of their deeds. I will kill her children with death, and all the churches shall know that I am He who searches the minds and hearts. And I will give to each one of you according to your works. Now to you I say, and to the rest in Thyatira, as many as do not have this doctrine, who have not known the depths of Satan, as they say, I will put on you no other burden."

The words that should be of concern are: "all the churches shall know that I am He who searches the minds and hearts." That which the "church" is and does, does not go unnoticed by The One Who is Head of the body (The Church). The words indicate there is an accountability factor. In the balance of these observations, Jesus makes clear that a "church" may continue to exist but the light-source will be removed from it. How do we know these things? Jesus Christ stated to the Apostle John, Revelation 1:17-29, "Do not be afraid; I am the

First and the Last. I am He who lives, and was dead, and behold, I am alive forevermore. Amen. And I have the keys of Hades and of Death. Write the things which you have seen, and the things which are, and the things which will take place after this. The mystery of the seven stars which you saw in My right hand, and the seven golden lamp-stands: The seven stars are the angels of the seven churches, and the seven lamp-stands which you saw are the seven churches." Jesus is abundantly clear in what he observes and He wants His Church to repent and be all of what He wants it to be – a spiritual bastion, a lighthouse whose light pierces the darkness, and that is engaged with the culture to declare the Gospel and the potential of one becoming a new creature – one who is more than a conqueror - in Christ Jesus.

FOR THOUGHT AND REFLECTION:

Why do you attend the "church" you have selected? Is it because of "programs" it offers? Is it because of denomination affiliation? Is it because you have friends who attend there?

In terms of Form and Function, do you attend a "church" because of its structural aesthetics? Is it because of the music – contemporary, traditional, or classical?

On a scale of one to ten, what should be the greatest priority of The Church you attend? Is it worship, music, preaching of the word, social activities, mission outreach, community outreach to the needy, or fellowship? Why?

How would you implement the "let us" principle of Hebrews 10:24 – "…let us consider one another…to stir up love and good works…" - in the "church" you attend?
What is your sense of the "church" you attend? Is it vibrant or boring?

Is the "worship" service meaningful or just time-consuming?

If you could make a change in the way your "church" functioned, what would it be?

What do you think is the cause of the following data/statistics: "In 2010, the following estimates were suggested: 1) 50% of the ministers starting out will not last 5 years; 2) 1 out of every 10 ministers will actually retire as a minister in some form; 3) 4,000 new churches begin each year and 7,000 churches close; 4) Over 1,700 pastors left the ministry every month last year; 5) Over 1,300 pastors were terminated by the local church each month, many without cause?

Do you think the above is a valid assessment of the "church" in our time? Why? Why not?

Jesus said: "…upon this rock I will build my church, and all the powers of hell will not conquer it."
Matthew 16:18 (NLT)

6. A Functional Profile

A "church" can be effective only if its members and attendees are serious regarding the authority and control of the Holy Spirit in their respective lives. A true follower of Jesus Christ will be submissive to the authority and control of the Holy Spirit and will also exhibit a discernible spiritual profile. For each follower of Jesus Christ, the issue of submission to the authority and control of the Holy Spirit is both basic and clear. Is the follower of Christ committed to and active in having an impact upon the culture of our day or is the follower of Christ lackadaisical and matter-of-fact regarding the subtleties of the culture and the impact it is having upon one? Another way of considering this issue is whether or not one is "A Cultural Conqueror" or allowing oneself to become "A Cultural Casualty"? While some will practice a straddle-the-fence approach to cultural matters, the end result is that the "church" has lost its voice and influence in an increasingly decadent society. Is it too late to shift gears and take your rightful place in the cultural conflict? One would hope not! However, to move one from complacency to highly motivated will require a major transformation and a greater commitment. The clock is ticking and an emphasis in Scripture needs to be heeded, II Corinthians 6:1-2, "We then, as workers together with Him also plead with you not to receive the grace of God in vain. For He says: In an acceptable time I have heard you, and in the day of salvation I have helped you. Behold, now is the accepted time; behold, now is the day of salvation." The emphasis is today is the day and now is the time. Will you be among those who respond immediately to the need of the day and hour in which we are living?

In a very urgent time in the life of the church, when it was being scattered and persecuted, Peter established how the Christian should live and function. In II Peter 1:1-4, he reminds those of like precious faith to remember the basic values and truths of Godly living regardless of the circumstances in which one may be surrounded. He wrote, "Simon Peter, a bondservant and apostle of Jesus Christ, To those who have obtained like precious faith with us by the righteousness of our God and Savior Jesus Christ: Grace and peace be multiplied to you in the knowledge of God and of Jesus our Lord, as His divine power has given to us all things that pertain to life and godliness, through the knowledge of Him who called us by glory and virtue, by which have been given to us exceedingly great and precious promises, that through these you may be partakers of the divine nature, having escaped the corruption that is in the world through lust."

The key thrust in these opening verses is: (1) His divine power has given to us all things that pertain to life and godliness. In other words, any secular power or assertions are unequal to His Divine power. Life and godliness do not need to be compromised because of any pressure by a decadent culture. (2) He has also given to us exceedingly great and precious promises, that through these you may be partakers of the divine nature. In other words, the divine nature is to be prominent in our lives as we remain and abide upon the exceedingly great and precious promises of God. An old Hymn of the Church that has been sung by many generations of church-goers is: Standing On The Promises of God, written in 1886 by R. Kelso Carter. The second stanza contains these words:

> Standing on the promises that cannot fail,
> When the howling storms of doubt and fear assail,
> By the living Word of God I shall prevail,
> Standing on the promises of God.

A parody of this hymn's premise has been made and suggests that too many who sing the words Standing on the Promises may actually be Sitting (or Sleeping) on the Premises. The question is obvious: Are you standing squarely and unflinchingly upon the exceedingly great and precious promises of God? If so, then the following must be true of you, namely (3) through these promises you are a partaker of the divine nature, having escaped the corruption that is in the world through lust. Verses 1 through 4 are foundational. If the follower of Christ is to endure the hardships of being scattered and persecuted, he/she must uncompromisingly understand what it is (a) to be a partaker of the divine nature, and (b) to escape the corruption that is in the world through lust. When one escapes the corruption, one is a conqueror. If one enjoys or is enslaved by the corruption, one is a casualty. There is no middle or neutral ground in terms of life-choice and/or one's functional profile.

Those truths being said, understood and applied, Peter instructs further what it means to live in a corrupt and decadent culture. In II Peter 1:5-11, Peter establishes the minimum functional profile for the follower of Christ when he writes: "But also for this very reason, giving all diligence, add to your faith virtue, to virtue knowledge, to knowledge self-control, to self-control perseverance, to perseverance godliness, to godliness brotherly kindness, and to brotherly kindness love. For if these things are yours and abound, you will be neither barren nor unfruitful in the knowledge of our Lord Jesus Christ. For he who lacks these things is shortsighted, even to blindness, and has forgotten that he was cleansed from his old sins. Therefore, brethren, be even more diligent to make your call and election sure, for if you do these things you will never stumble; for so an entrance will be supplied to you abundantly into the everlasting kingdom of our Lord and Savior Jesus Christ."

What is the Functional Profile for the follower of Christ? It begins with an understanding and appreciation of The Qualities and Attributes of the Believer. The profile's beginning point is based upon II Corinthians 5:17, "Therefore, if anyone is in Christ, he is a new creation; old things have passed away; behold, all things have become new." The statement of Paul is clear, the old is passing away and all things are becoming new. Actually, it is the work of sanctification that has begun and is in process wherein one dies more and more unto sin/self and lives more and more unto God/Holiness. The New Living Translation of II Corinthians 5:17-18(a) is: "What this means is that those who become Christians become new persons. They are not the same anymore, for the old life is gone. A new life has begun! All this newness of life is from God, who brought us back to himself through what Christ did." The old self being gone does not mean one now exists in a vacuum. Life has not become meaningless but rather meaningful. The old things that were so detrimental to one have been removed and new things are starting to inhabit one's spiritual being.

Those things that are to be added to one's life should be understood as: Seven Qualities/Attributes to Be Added to One's Faith. The fact that these Qualities and Attributes are to be added means that one cannot pick and choose which qualities one wishes to have and which ones can be set aside. Each Quality or Attribute is connected with every other Quality and Attribute. It begins with faith and then:

(1) Add to your faith virtue. Virtue is the moral power, moral energy, and invigorates soul.

(2) Add to virtue knowledge. Knowledge is the insight and understanding one gains in his/her walk of faith. It entails coming to know God more fully and Jesus Christ more completely. It includes knowing His will, plan, and purpose for one's life. It is suggested that Epaphras may have been the Pastor of the Church in Laodicea and Hierapolis. What is significant is the prayer that he offered in their behalf - Colossians 4:12-13(a): "Epaphras, who is one of you, a bondservant of Christ, greets you, always laboring fervently for you in prayers, that you may

stand perfect and complete in all the will of God. For I bear him witness that he has a great zeal for you..."

(3) Add to knowledge self-control. Self-control means "to hold oneself in." An example of this meaning is in the requirement for a church Elder given in Titus 1:6-9, "if a man is blameless, the husband of one wife, having faithful children not accused of dissipation or insubordination. For a bishop must be blameless, as a steward of God, not self-willed, not quick-tempered, not given to wine, not violent, not greedy for money, but hospitable, a lover of what is good, sober-minded, just, holy, self-controlled, holding fast the faithful word as he has been taught, that he may be able, by sound doctrine, both to exhort and convict those who contradict." The word "bishop" is interchangeable with the word "elder". Two areas that stand out in terms of this Quality are: (a) not self-willed, and (b) one who maintains self-control at all times and in all situations. It may be challenging from time to time but it serves as a refining process both in and for us.

(4) Add to self-control, perseverance. Perseverance indicates one must have patience in all things and with all people. The reality is that one's perseverance will be tested from time to time. The more one wishes to pursue and prevail in terms of perseverance the greater some pressure will come to bear upon one's life and practice. Paul indicates this in Romans 5:3-4, "...but we also glory in tribulations, knowing that tribulation produces perseverance; and perseverance, character; and character, hope." As difficult as tribulations are and will be, we should not

dread them. We know that it is part of the process wherein one is being conformed to the image of Christ.

(5) Add to perseverance, godliness. How does one achieve godliness? II Peter 1:3 indicated: "His divine power has given us everything we need for life and godliness through our knowledge of him who called us by his own glory and goodness." We need to be focused and receptive to what God's divine power is making available to us, namely, "...everything we need for life and godliness through our knowledge of him who called us by his own glory and goodness." Everything we need for life and godliness! Nothing has been withheld! Everything is at one's disposal! Not some things, but everything! Godliness becomes an increasing reality as one humbles himself under the mighty hand of God and seeks His face continually. It is the embrace and action of a total commitment to Jesus Christ and God's will for one's life.

(6) Add to godliness, brotherly kindness. Brotherly kindness is a deliberate and disciplined action and activity. It is the embrace and commitment to Ephesians 4:30-32, "And do not grieve the Holy Spirit of God, by whom you were sealed for the day of redemption. Let all bitterness, wrath, anger, clamor, and evil speaking be put away from you, with all malice. And be kind to one another, tenderhearted, forgiving one another, just as God in Christ forgave you." It is also the realization that if this is not occurring continually in one's life, then the Holy Spirit is grieved. The negatives must be surrendered and removed and the positives must fill and saturate one's mind, emotions and

will. Anything short of that grieves the Holy Spirit of God. The follower of Christ must be kind to others, tenderhearted, maintaining a forgiving spirit and implementing it by one's behavior. It also means one must keep himself free from anger, animosity, hatred and the desire and drive for retaliation. Can the follower of Christ do these things? Not in one's own strength! However, the love, mercy and grace of God can effectuate these qualities and attributes in and through you.

(7) Add to brotherly kindness, love. It means one is to give heed to the words of Jesus Christ when He said to the enquiring lawyer in Luke 10:27-28, "So he (the lawyer) answered and said: You shall love the Lord your God with all your heart, with all your soul, with all your strength, and with all your mind, and your neighbor as yourself. And He (Jesus) said to him, you have answered rightly; do this and you will live." The bottom line for a functional profile is that one must love the Lord with all of his heart, soul, strength and mind. Additionally, one must also love his neighbor as himself, as well as loving one's enemies and praying for those who are doing the scattering and persecuting. What is the level of love one is to show and by which one is to be motivated? It is the same type of love with which God so loved the world and gave His only-begotten Son. It is an agape love that is genuine and intense. This is how God loved us and He expects us to emulate Him by showing the reality of His love in and through us who follow Him.

Too often, rationalization enters in where responsible action should occur. The lawyer was a man of considerable wealth and was reluctant to become involved. Note how the discussion raises an additional question in Luke 10:29-37, "But he (the lawyer), wanting to justify himself, said to Jesus, And who is my neighbor? Then Jesus answered and said: A certain man went down from Jerusalem to Jericho, and fell among thieves, who stripped him of his clothing, wounded him, and departed, leaving him half dead. Now by chance a certain priest came down that road. And when he saw him, he passed by on the other side. Likewise a Levite, when he arrived at the place, came and looked, and passed by on the other side. But a certain Samaritan, as he journeyed, came where he was. And when he saw him, he had compassion. So he went to him and bandaged his wounds, pouring on oil and wine; and he set him on his own animal, brought him to an inn, and took care of him. On the next day, when he departed, he took out two *denarii*, gave them to the innkeeper, and said to him, Take care of him; and whatever more you spend, when I come again, I will repay you. So which of these three do you think was neighbor to him who fell among the thieves? And he said, He who showed mercy on him. Then Jesus said to him, Go and do likewise."

For a brief moment, let us consider who it was who was moved with compassion, mercy and financial commitment. Was it the Priest? No! Was it the Levite? No! It was one who's only identity was "a certain Samaritan." What is significant about "a certain Samaritan" being responsive to the plight and need of the "certain man" who was left for dead by a band of thieves? There is an interesting observation and application made in the

Matthew Henry Concise Commentary. Most would not think of "a certain Samaritan" responding to anyone of the Jewish people. Why? Because Samaritans were despised, ostracized and avoided by a large portion of the Jewish nation. Matthew Henry suggests: "...a Samaritan, of the nation which the Jews most despised and detested, and would have no dealings with. It is lamentable to observe how selfishness governs all ranks; how many excuses men will make to avoid trouble or expense in relieving others. But the true Christian has the law of love written in his heart. The Spirit of Christ dwells in him; Christ's image is renewed in his soul. The parable is a beautiful explanation of the law of loving our neighbor as ourselves, without regard to nation, party, or any other distinction. It also sets forth the kindness and love of God our Savior toward sinful, miserable men. We were like this poor, distressed traveler. Satan, our enemy, has robbed us, and wounded us: such is the mischief sin has done us. The blessed Jesus had compassion on us. The believer considers that Jesus loved him, and gave his life for him, when an enemy and a rebel; and having shown him mercy, he bids him go and do likewise. It is the duty of us all along our pathway in life and according to our ability, to succor, help, and relieve all who are in distress and necessity." Surely, the follower of Christ should never allow for cultural biases to interfere with ministry and service done in Jesus' name.

    If the follower of Christ is serious about relationship and commitment to Jesus Christ, he/she will discover that the promises of God will sustain one regardless of how others may respond. There may be times when one feels isolated and all alone in the cultural conflict. A man as great and significant as Elijah had such a moment. He had become frustrated and dejected as he feared for his life. In I Kings 19:13-14, The Lord asks Elijah a question: "What are you doing here, Elijah?" Elijah, without hesitation, states his frustration, dejection and fear: "I have been very zealous for the Lord God of hosts; because the children of Israel have forsaken Your covenant, torn down Your altars, and killed Your prophets with the sword. I alone am left; and they seek to take my life." As the text progresses, it's almost as though the Lord is saying to Elijah, "Get over it." One gets this sense from I Kings 19:15-16, "Then the Lord said to him: Go, return on your way to the Wilderness of Damascus; and when you arrive, anoint Hazael as king over Syria. Also you shall anoint Jehu the son of Nimshi as king over Israel. And Elisha the son of Shaphat of Abel Meholah you shall anoint as prophet in your place." The Lord is saying to His servant that He is in control over the what and when of one's life. For Elijah, He was informing him that his task was not yet completed in the cultural conflict of his day. And then, serving almost as a post script, the Lord states in I Kings 19:18, oh, by the way Elijah, "I have reserved seven thousand in Israel, all whose knees have not bowed to Baal, and every mouth that has not kissed him." The Lord is essentially saying: get over your dejection, frustration and fear; do your assignment; I am still with you and will guide you and keep you until I take you to My Heaven.

What is your response and reaction when you seem overwhelmed with the sense of being alone or forgotten? It is easy to observe some who profess to be a follower of Christ given to despair, fear and uncertainty. There are times when one is reminded of a segment on the old Hee-Haw program where a song would be sung: "Gloom, despair and agony on me; Deep, dark depression, excessive misery; If it weren't for bad luck, I'd have no luck at all; Gloom, despair and agony on me." For those who easily wring their hands and move into a type of despair with the News – and every nuance of it – whether it is a looming storm, or war, or a nation sliding down the slippery slope – there is a word from The Word. Hebrews 6:17-20 (NLT) states: "God also bound himself with an oath, so that those who received the promise could be perfectly sure that he would never change his mind. So God has given us both his promise and his oath. These two things are unchangeable because it is impossible for God to lie. Therefore, we who have fled to him for refuge can take new courage, for we can hold on to his promise with confidence (hope). This confidence (hope) is like a strong and trustworthy anchor for our souls. It leads us through the curtain of heaven into God's inner sanctuary. Jesus has already gone in there for us..." The song with which the professing follower of Jesus Christ should identify is: "My hope is in the Lord, Who gave Himself for me; and paid the price for all my sin, at Calvary." Another stanza has these words: "And now for me He stands, before the Father's throne; He shows is wounded hands and names me as His own." He alone is the source of one's life and the basis of one's hope.

It substantiates that one needs to be focused upon a faithful God and His promises to His followers. When it comes to such a focus on the promises of God and whether or not they will be both appropriate and functional in one's life, an anchor text one should remember is, II Corinthians 1:19-20, For the Son of God, Jesus Christ, who was preached among you by us...was not Yes and No, but in Him was Yes. For all the promises of God in Him are Yes, and in Him Amen, to the glory of God through us."

FOR THOUGHT AND REFLECTION:

In terms of the authority and control of the Holy Spirit in your life, how seriously do you consider and respond to the Holy Spirit?

Can you identify your walk in life in the same way Paul establishes in Galatians 5:16, "walk by the enablement of the Spirit..."?

In terms of a Spiritual Profile, does yours more reflect the fruit of the Spirit, or the desires of the flesh? Does this include all areas of your life? Why? Why not?

If there was an ethnic group who viewed you with suspicion and/or disdain, and there was an obvious need within that group, how would you respond?

Would you be like the Priest of Levite and ignore the obvious need? Or, would you be like the Samaritan and respond with kindness, compassion and mercy? Why? Why not?

Based upon the Lord's Parable in Luke 10, how should cross-cultural ministry in Jesus' name be approached and done by you and your church?

Should it be viewed as a missionary endeavor or as one in which the local church must be involved? Why? Why not?

How many promises of God do you know? What are they? Try to list seven (one for each day of the week).

Are these an anchor for your soul and a motivation for your personal involvement with the lost and needy? In this regard, share another promise you embrace!

What lesson(s) do you think Jesus wants us to learn from His ministry with a Samaritan in John 4?

Might you be misunderstood and criticized if you did as Jesus did?

Should that make any difference in terms of your personal ministry commitment?

Do you not say, There are still four months and then comes the harvest? Behold, I say to you, lift up your eyes and look at the fields, for they are already white for harvest! And he who reaps receives wages, and gathers fruit for eternal life, that both he who sows and he who reaps may rejoice together.
John 4:35-36 (NKJV)

7. Personal Engagement

Throughout history, there are always circumstances that arise that can easily be referred to as troubled times. It might be war, famine, persecution, ethnic cleansing, natural disasters – tsunamis, earthquakes, tornadoes – as well as fragile economies – recession and/or depression. In addition, moral values can be under attack and limitations may be imposed on Christian assertions and/or affirmations. What should the follower of Christ do at such times? Is this the time for putting on the whole armor of God and becoming fully engaged in the spiritual warfare that is occurring? What is the major weapon in one's arsenal for the battle at hand? Ephesians 6:17 states that one's weapon is to be "…the sword of the Spirit, which is the word of God…"

Amid The Cultural Chaos and a spiritual revolt, the Gospel remains as the tremendous equalizer. In Romans 1:16, Paul indicates that the Gospel "…is the power of God to salvation for everyone who believes…" the word translated "power" is the Greek word *dunamis* upon which a current usage is "dynamite" (although in the first century, dynamite was not the frame of reference). The Gospel has application and includes rich and poor; educated and non-educated; significant and insignificant; successful or failures; Jew or Gentile – all stand before Jesus Christ on equal footing and common ground. The pericope - Romans 3:10-24 - states God's basis upon which this occurs: "There is none righteous, no, not one; there is none who understands; there is none who seeks after God. They have all turned aside; they have together become unprofitable; there is none who does good, no, not one. Their throat is an open tomb; with their tongues they have practiced deceit; the poison of asps is under their lips; whose mouth is full of cursing and bitterness. Their feet are swift to shed blood; destruction and misery are in their ways; and the way of peace they have not known. There is no fear of God before their eyes. Now we know that whatever the law says, it says to those who are under the law, that every mouth may be stopped, and all the world may become guilty before God. Therefore by the deeds of the law no flesh will be justified in His sight, for by the law is the knowledge of sin. But now the righteousness of God apart from the law is revealed, being witnessed by the Law and the Prophets, even the righteousness of God, through faith in Jesus Christ, to all and on all who believe. For there is no difference; for all have sinned and fall short of the glory of God, being justified freely by His grace through the redemption that is in Christ Jesus."

The establishment of a relationship with the Savior is paramount. Paul shared this same emphasis when he expressed it in Galatians 3:26-29 (NIV), "You are all sons of God through faith in Christ Jesus, for all of you who were baptized into Christ have clothed yourselves with Christ. There is neither Jew nor Greek, slave nor free, male nor female, for you are all one in Christ Jesus. If you belong to Christ, then you are Abraham's seed, and heirs according to the promise." The relationship involves at least two important factors: (1) the relationship is with Jesus

Christ and growth in Him must occur; and (2) The Covenant of Promise is a reality for the follower of Jesus Christ.

Too often within the "church", a subtle "pecking-order" evolves. This can occur for a multitude of reasons. The reasons are not the focus for discussion here but the motivations of those who allow for the prominence of some and the insignificance of others is the focus. Why should a person of wealth have greater prominence and influence over one who may be impoverished? Why should a social-elite receive greater recognition and preference over one who is seen as common and ordinary? Why should a person of academic excellence have greater status than one who never completed high school? A passage of Scripture that addresses these considerations is fascinating. In I Corinthians 1:17-31, we read: "For Christ did not send me to baptize, but to preach the gospel--not with words of human wisdom, lest the cross of Christ be emptied of its power. For the message of the cross is foolishness to those who are perishing, but to us who are being saved it is the power of God. For it is written: I will destroy the wisdom of the wise; the intelligence of the intelligent I will frustrate. Where is the wise man? Where is the scholar? Where is the philosopher of this age? Has not God made foolish the wisdom of the world? For since in the wisdom of God the world through its wisdom did not know him, God was pleased through the foolishness of what was preached to save those who believe. Jews demand miraculous signs and Greeks look for wisdom, but we preach Christ crucified: a stumbling block to Jews and foolishness to Gentiles, but to those whom

God has called, both Jews and Greeks, Christ the power of God and the wisdom of God. For the foolishness of God is wiser than man's wisdom, and the weakness of God is stronger than man's strength. Brothers, think of what you were when you were called. Not many of you were wise by human standards; not many were influential; not many were of noble birth. But God chose the foolish things of the world to shame the wise; God chose the weak things of the world to shame the strong. He chose the lowly things of this world and the despised things--and the things that are not--to nullify the things that are, so that no one may boast before him. It is because of him that you are in Christ Jesus, who has become for us wisdom from God, that is, our righteousness, holiness and redemption. Therefore, as it is written: Let him who boasts boast in the Lord."

When these truths are grasped, it should begin to make a difference in terms of how we relate to each other within the "church" and then as the "church" extends itself into the community and world. The common ground is oneness in Christ where personal distinctions and preferences are of no importance or validity. It may not always be exhibited or practiced in a community "church". Even if that is one's experience or frustration, one can seek out ways and situations in which one can be personally engaged in ministry for the Lord. It must also be remembered that the follower of Christ is serving the Lord, not men! What are some of the personal engagements in which one may participate or generate? If the "church" has become static or stagnant, what can and should a committed follower of Christ do?

A starting point is found in the "let us" passages in Hebrews. This phrase envisions a concerted commitment by like-minded people. It conveys a corporate rather than an individualistic approach. There should never be an excuse allowed that would cause avoidance of one's personal engagement in ministry. There may be times when one may feel and/or be alone in a cause and stand for righteousness. One can manage that experience and situation by remembering one of the "let us" factors that must be part of one's thinking and ministry effort, namely, Hebrews 12:2, (let us be) "…looking unto Jesus, the Author and Finisher of our faith." What one does and/or is doing is for Him and His glory – not for self-gratification or recognition.

There are at least fifteen "let us" references and inferences in Hebrews. Most of them are clearly stated as hortatory subjunctives (grammatically - a statement urging others to join in some action; commanding oneself and one's associates and always translated as "let us").They are: (1) Hebrews 4:1 – "since a promise remains of entering His rest, let us fear lest any of you seem to have come short of it." (2) Hebrews 4:11 – "Let us therefore be diligent to enter that rest." (3) Hebrews 4:14 – "let us hold fast our confession." (4) Hebrews 4:15 – "Let us therefore come boldly to the throne of grace." (5) Hebrews 6:1 – "let us go on to perfection." (6) Hebrews 10:22 – "let us draw near with a true heart in full assurance of faith." (7) Hebrews 10:23 – "Let us hold fast the confession of our hope without wavering."

(8) Hebrews 10:24 - "let us consider one another in order to stir up love and good works." (9) Hebrews 10:25 – (let us) "not forsake the assembling of ourselves together." (10) Hebrews 10:25 – (let us be) "exhorting one another." (11) Hebrews 12:1 - "let us lay aside every weight and the sin which so easily ensnares us." (12) Hebrews 12:1 - "let us run with endurance the race that is set before us." (13) Hebrews 12:2 – (let us be) "looking unto Jesus." (14) Hebrews 13:13 – "let us go forth to Him, outside the camp, bearing His reproach." (15) Hebrews 13:15 – "by Him let us continually offer the sacrifice of praise to God."

While all of these declarations need to be embraced and implemented, one "let us" reference that should always remember is, Hebrews 10:23 – "Let us hold fast the confession of our hope without wavering." The phrases that should be underscored in one's thinking and practice are: (a) hold fast, (b) the confession of your hope, and (c) without wavering. The phrase "hold fast" linguistically is a present active volitive subjunctive that emphasizes "keep on holding fast." The thought being conveyed is for one to cling to the faith one has professed and remain confident as one clings to the hope in the soul without wavering. It reminds one of a previous truth given in Hebrews 6:17-20 (ESV), "So when God desired to show more convincingly to the heirs of the promise the unchangeable character of his purpose, he guaranteed it with an oath, so that by two unchangeable things, in which it is impossible for God to lie, we who have fled for refuge might have strong encouragement to hold fast to the hope set before us. We have this as a sure and steadfast anchor of the soul, a hope that enters into the inner place behind the curtain, where Jesus has gone as a forerunner on our behalf." One should "keep on holding fast" and to remember that in one's relationship with the Lord one is enabled to realize "we have an anchor of the soul, sure and steadfast." It enables one to experience a unique reality, namely, being in the Presence of one's Lord and Savior. This should translate into a deeper and more intimate relationship to the Lord.

In his treatise on the subject of The Practice of the Presence of God, Brother Lawrence wrote: "In the practice of the presence of God we call Our Father to mind at every possible moment. At every opportunity, we focus our attention on Him. We should feed and nourish our soul with high notions of God which yield us great joy in being devoted to Him." As one enters into this practice, it will strengthen one to keep on holding fast, and to have a confident hope as an anchor for the soul, and to do so without wavering or doubt. This is basic and essential for the one who wants to be personally engaged in ministry for the Lord. An empty vessel has nothing to share with the thirsty soul. To be engaged in the practice of the presence of God will require a daily diligence and discipline. Lesser things should not gain one's attention or be allowed to distract from the commitment and goal of one's life, namely, to be fully aware of all that it means to live one's life in the presence of God.

The culture in which we live and where we should be ministering has allowed for a departure from the things that are basic for the soul. If one is not developing and growing in Christ, he/she will easily and quickly become a cultural prey. Rather than being "A Cultural Conqueror" and positive presence, one will become "A Cultural Casualty" and sidelined. An illustration of this cultural tension is evidence in the days of Noah. Genesis 6 states "Noah walked with God." In that walk with God, Genesis 6:11-13 indicates: "The earth also was corrupt before God, and the earth was filled with violence. So God looked upon the earth, and indeed it was corrupt; for all flesh had corrupted their way on the earth. And God said to Noah: The end of all flesh has come before Me, for the earth is filled with violence through them; and behold, I will destroy them with the earth." The tension is one walking with God while living "Amid The Cultural Chaos" and the overwhelming majority not walking with God.

How was Noah, the righteous man viewed by a corrupt culture? Hebrews 11:7 gives a brief summary about Noah, "By faith Noah, being divinely warned of things not yet seen, moved with godly fear, prepared an ark for the saving of his household, by which he condemned the world and became heir of the righteousness which is according to faith." Peter echoes the summary about Noah, in II Peter 2:4-5, "For if God did not spare the angels who sinned, but cast them down to hell and delivered them into chains of darkness, to be reserved for judgment; and did not spare the ancient world, but saved Noah, one of eight people, a preacher of righteousness, bringing in the flood on the world of the ungodly." The preacher and doer of righteousness was ignored by the culture of his day. He was mocked and derided for being a foolish man as he built a large ark for a refuge against an impending flood. There hadn't been a heavy rainfall or flooding conditions during the years of his building the ark. The culture had no spiritual reference point about God, or judgment, or floods. It became easy to ignore and ridicule Noah. After all, he was clearly out of touch with reality and the culture of his day. He didn't fit in with the cultural norm. Essentially, he is a model and demonstration of what it means to keep on holding fast; keep on having hope as an anchor for the soul; and keep on doing one's assigned work without wavering or doubting before God.

The culture has never been a friend to righteousness and holiness. The task for the follower of Christ is formidable. If you're tempted to feel that you're alone and become afraid, be reminded of those who are mentioned in Hebrews 11. There is a special group mentioned who are unknown and unnamed. They are referred to as the "still others" in Hebrews 11:36-38 (ESV), "Still others suffered mocking and flogging, and even chains and imprisonment. They were stoned, they were sawn in two, they were killed with the sword. They went about in skins of sheep and goats, destitute, afflicted, mistreated - of whom the world was not worthy - wandering about in deserts and mountains, and in dens and caves of the earth." That might represent any one of us in the culture and times in which we live – unknown and unnamed – but with the epitaph of God, "of whom the world was not worthy." Regardless of the turmoil in the world or the personal upheaval one may experience, there must be the commitment to keep on holding fast, with a confident hope as an anchor for one's soul, and doing so without wavering or vacillating. Are we among the "let us" being referenced here? Is your identity with the "still others" who remained faithful to the end?

As one becomes personally engaged in ministry within the culture that has been able to influence and impact the lives of many, the task will involve rescue and recovery. It is to be engaged at a level indicated in Jude 14-23, "Behold, the Lord comes with ten thousands of His saints, to execute judgment on all, to convict all who are ungodly among them of all their ungodly deeds which they have committed in an ungodly way, and of all the harsh things which ungodly sinners have spoken against Him. These are grumblers, complainers, walking according to their own lusts; and they mouth great swelling words, flattering people to gain advantage. But you, beloved, remember the words which were spoken before by the apostles of our Lord Jesus Christ: how they told you that there would be mockers in the last time who would walk according to their own ungodly lusts. These are sensual persons, who cause divisions, not having the Spirit. But you, beloved, building yourselves up on your most holy faith, praying in the Holy Spirit, keep yourselves in the love of God, looking for the mercy of our Lord Jesus Christ unto eternal life. And on some have compassion, making a distinction; but others save with fear, pulling them out of the fire, hating even the garment defiled by the flesh."

Matthew Henry's Concise Commentary addresses verse 17-23, "Sensual men separate from Christ, and his church, and join themselves to the devil, the world, and the flesh, by ungodly and sinful practices. That is infinitely worse than to separate from any branch of the visible church on account of opinions, or modes and circumstances of outward government or worship. Sensual men have not the spirit of holiness, which whoever has not, does not belong to Christ. The grace of faith is most holy, as it works by love, purifies the heart, and overcomes the world, by which it is distinguished from a false and dead faith. Our prayers are most likely to prevail, when we pray in the Holy Ghost, under his guidance and influence, according to the rule of his word, with faith, fervency, and earnestness; this is praying in the Holy Ghost. And a believing expectation of eternal life will arm us against the snares of sin: lively faith in this blessed hope will help us to mortify our lusts. We must watch over one another; faithfully, yet prudently reprove each other, and set a good example to all about us. This must be done with compassion, making a difference between the weak and the willful. Some we must treat with tenderness. Others save with fear; urging the terrors of the Lord. All endeavors must be joined with decided abhorrence of crimes, and care be taken to avoid whatever led to, or was connected with fellowship with them, in works of darkness, keeping far from what is, or appears to be evil."

    This is a daunting task that will require discipline, perseverance and reliance upon the power of God. The battle is not against a flesh and blood enemy but one that entails conflict on a spiritual level that is intense. Ephesians 6:12-13 (ESV) indicates the battle in which the follower of Christ is engaged: "For our struggle is not against flesh and blood, but against the rulers, against the authorities, against the powers of this dark world and against the spiritual forces of evil in the heavenly realms. Therefore put on the full armor of God, so that when the day of evil comes, you may be able to stand your ground, and after you have done everything, to stand." In the midst of this conflict for the souls of men, keep a focus on those who are often overlooked or passed by. There needs to be a recognition regarding those who desperately need someone to come alongside of them and to give a word of encouragement and direction. Too often, a form of child abuse is when one's body language or attitude conveys to an individual that they lack anything of merit; or have no value or self-worth; or will never amount to anything. One can only wonder if this is a contributing factor to teenage suicide. In one study done in 2006, the report stated: "Teenage suicide in the United States remains comparatively high in the 15 to 24 age group with 4,299 suicides in this age range in 2004, making it the third leading cause of death for those aged 15 to 24. By comparison, suicide is the 11th leading cause of death for all those age 10 and over, with 33,289 suicides for all US citizens..." One teenager recently wrote, "I try and try and try and everything I do is wrong. From now on, I just don't exist anymore." There are a lot of people who feel that way about themselves. Some take a fatal step by taking their own life and departing from their context of non-acceptance and insignificance. In pain, one becomes a suicide statistic. The lament, usually too late is: "I had no idea…" or "If I had only known…" These are copout phrases one uses to excuse oneself for not being concerned, or responsible to invest in and make a difference in another's life. If you had an idea and/or if you had only known, what would you have done differently? What preventative effort would you have made? A person submitted a Post on Facebook, October 21, 2013: "A weird, sad experience this afternoon. Walking the alley to the recycling dumpster, I see a van, engine on, hose from exhaust up and through passenger window. Call 911. Doors locked. Music inside. Tinted windows…can't see anyone inside. Finally get a door open, turn engine off. Young lady in the back unconscious. Take key, open van doors. Run get Nurse Jan. She works to get the gal awake. EMT, police arrive. All is ok. The lady herself says she's ok. Cop says she'll be taken to hospital. Ambulance leaves. Neighbor says I saved a life. I'm ready to cry. So much pain. She needs Jesus. Where will this end? How will she meet Jesus?" What would you have done if you had approached the Van? With this and other similar circumstances, how would you have responded? Would you have ignored it? This is the rescue and recovery task we have been given by Jesus Christ as we minister in His name to a culture that despises Him and His standards. He expects us to do it. He doesn't want to hear our excuse for not getting involved. Don't become a casualty. Go forward being one who is more than a conqueror through Him Who loved us.

FOR THOUGHT AND REFLECTION:

How would you describe your concern for and involvement in ministry with the culture of our day? What is your personal sense of the depth of need? Define it!

Do you measure your personal concern for others in terms of their ethnic origins; or social strata; or intellectual status; or financial influence? Why?

In your own personal life, would you describe it as one that has a positive influence upon the culture or that you have been negatively impacted by the culture?

If you make a commitment to be personally engaged in ministry and you are rejected in your effort, what should your response and reaction be? Should you retaliate? Should you re-group and try again? Why? Why not?

Do you have a mistaken notion that your "church" and the "paid professional" (the Pastor) is supposed to be engaged in this spiritual conflict for the souls and minds of people?

If you could identify one thing that would prevent you from indiscriminate outreach ministry, what would that one thing be?

Are you afraid of failure or rejection if you implement personal engagement within our culture?

Do you think Jesus and His disciples succeeded or failed in their ministry efforts? Why?

Have you ever been acquainted with one who either attempted suicide and/or successfully committed suicide? What was your feeling afterwards? Is there anything you could have or should have tried to do? If yes, what would that anything be?

Inasmuch as those who return from extended military duty, as well as teenagers, are a high percentile of those who attempt and/or succeed in committing suicide, what possible "target group" should be a priority for you? Should you merely pray for them? Should you make a donation to a veteran's group or some teen program? Should you be personally involved in reaching out to them?

Then the King will say to those on his right, Come, you who are blessed by my Father; take your inheritance, the kingdom prepared for you since the creation of the world. For I was hungry and you gave me something to eat, I was thirsty and you gave me something to drink, I was a stranger and you invited me in, I needed clothes and you clothed me, I was sick and you looked after me, I was in prison and you came to visit me. Then the righteous will answer him, 'Lord, when did we see you hungry and feed you, or thirsty and give you something to drink? When did we see you a stranger and invite you in, or needing clothes and clothe you? When did we see you sick or in prison and go to visit you? The King will reply, I tell you the truth, whatever you did for one of the least of these brothers of mine, you did for me.
Matthew 25:34-40 (NIV)

8. The Risks of Personal Engagement

The Bible contains several examples of the risk potential when one is personally engaged in adhering to God's Standards and attempting to implement a God-consciousness within one's culture. The examples demonstrate everything from bitter envy, such as Cain despising Abel, through the Crucifixion of Jesus Christ when hostile mobs chose a criminal rather than the Messiah, and throughout the persecutions of the first century up to and including the twenty-first century.

More than a decade ago, John Piper submitted on the Desiring God webpage an article entitled: A Call For Christian Risk. He wrote: "By removing eternal risk, Christ calls his people to continual temporal risk. For the followers of Jesus the final risk is gone. There is now no condemnation for those who are in Christ Jesus (Romans 8:1). Neither death nor life…will be able to separate us from the love of God in Christ Jesus our Lord (Romans 3:38-39). Some of you they will put to death…But not a hair of your head will perish (Luke 21:16, 18). Whoever believes in me, though he die, yet shall he live (John 11:25). When a Christian says from the heart, to live is Christ and to die is gain, he is free to love no matter what…In America and around the world the price of being a real Christian is rising. Increasingly II Timothy 3:12 will make sense: All who desire to live a godly life in Christ Jesus will be persecuted. Those who've made gospel-risk a voluntary life-style will be most ready when we have no choice. Therefore I urge you, in the words of the early church, Let us go to him outside the camp and bear the reproach he endured. For here we have no lasting city, but we seek the city that is to come (Hebrews 13:13-14)."

Among the Biblical examples of risk taking and risk management, one that immediately comes to mind is the account of Gideon and his three hundred faithful men. Their challenge was considerable and their prospect for victory was not certain. In order to know whether or not they would be successful and victorious, they would have to believe the impossible was possible. The Midianites were a formidable foe and threat to the children of Israel. We get a clear sense of this in Judges 6:6, "So Israel was greatly impoverished because of the Midianites, and the children of Israel cried out to the Lord." While the Midianites were wreaking havoc among the children of Israel, the Lord was in the process of selecting His man to do His work in His way. The Lord makes His choice. His man for the task is Gideon. In Judges 6:12-16 (ESV), "And the angel of the Lord appeared to him and said to him: The Lord is with you, O mighty man of valor. And Gideon said to him, Please, sir, if the Lord is with us, why then has all this happened to us? And where are all his wonderful deeds that our fathers recounted to us, saying, Did not the Lord bring us up from Egypt?' But now the Lord has forsaken us and given us into the hand of Midian. And the Lord turned to him and said, Go in this might of yours and save Israel from the hand of Midian; do not I send you? And he said to him, Please, Lord, how can I save Israel? Behold, my clan is the weakest in

Manasseh, and I am the least in my father's house. And the Lord said to him: But I will be with you, and you shall strike the Midianites as one man."

The response of Gideon to the call of God is similar to how many individuals throughout history have replied. It's as though one dares to say to the Lord: "It can't be me! You need someone else for the task." Gideon responded to the Lord's direction: "O my Lord, how can I save Israel? Indeed my clan is the weakest in Manasseh, and I am the least in my father's house." This is not a false sense of humility but a sense of inadequacy. One is always more apt to assess a task or challenge in terms of the human element and one's physical ability rather than being aware of God's power that is available and at work within the follower of Jesus Christ.

After Gideon responds to God's call, he has not yet been made aware of how great his challenge will be. Even though he had recruited an army to join him in the battle against the Midianites, the Lord had a different plan for Gideon. In Judges 7:2-7, Gideon will learn what it is: "And the Lord said to Gideon, The people who are with you are too many for Me to give the Midianites into their hands, lest Israel claim glory for itself against Me, saying, My own hand has saved me. Now therefore, proclaim in the hearing of the people, saying: Whoever is fearful and afraid, let him turn and depart at once from Mount Gilead. And twenty-two-thousand of the people returned, and ten thousand remained. But the Lord said to Gideon, The people are still too many; bring them down to the water, and I will test them for you there. Then it will be, that of whom I say to you: This one shall go with you, the same shall go with you; and of whomever I say to you: This one shall not go with you, the same shall not go. So he brought the people down to the water. And the Lord said to Gideon, Everyone who laps from the water with his tongue, as a dog laps, you shall set apart by himself; likewise everyone who gets down on his knees to drink. And the number of those who lapped, putting their hand to their mouth, was three hundred men; but all the rest of the people got down on their knees to drink water. Then the Lord said to Gideon: By the three hundred men who lapped I will save you, and deliver the Midianites into your hand. Let all the other people go, every man to his place."

Think of it – an army of thirty-thousand men is reduced to three-hundred. This is beginning to look like a suicide mission. Will this small group prevail against the formidable army aligned against Israel? The Lord's statement regarding the reduction of the army is: "...lest Israel claim glory for itself against Me, saying, my own hand has saved me." This is a vital lesson one must learn when endeavoring to do the will of God. We serve at the Lord's command and we trust Him to be The One Who enables us to do the task He has assigned. Will it challenge us to pursue a goal previously unknown to us? Yes! Will we be able to finish the task and journey well? Yes! Will we be stretched beyond what our perceived human ability is believed to be? Yes! The answer is given in Judges 8:4 where there was not only the risk factor but also the fatigue factor indicated. As the enemy is being pursued, the text indicates their physical condition: "When Gideon came to the Jordan, he and the three hundred men who were with him crossed over, exhausted but still in pursuit." What a beautiful statement and an apt motto for one's life: "exhausted but still in pursuit." Some translations use the word "faint" in place of "exhausted." The picture is one of men who had exerted themselves to the maximum in order that they might accomplish their mission for the Lord.

As we weigh the risk-factor when endeavoring to serve the Lord, there is an account of the Jerusalem Council making a decision for extended ministry in Acts 15:24-26 (NIV). The Council stated: "We have heard that some went out from us without our authorization and disturbed you, troubling your minds by what they said. So we all agreed to choose some men and send them to you with our dear friends Barnabas and Paul - men who have risked their lives for the name of our Lord Jesus Christ." There are two factors suggested and stated here, namely (1) men of integrity and accuracy were being sent, and (2) their character was apparent because they were known and respected as "...men who have risked their lives for the name of our Lord Jesus Christ." An interesting phrase in these verses is stated in the past tense, namely, "have risked their lives." The fact is that as they go forth on their mission they will be risking their lives many more times. Risk has become a pattern of their lives. They are engaged in an ongoing spiritual warfare and it will not be abated in one's lifetime. As they engage in this warfare, they will continue to face challenges, opposition, conflicts, imprisonments and persecutions. The men were chosen because they were known for their endurance and dependability. It should also be noted that they did not always know when they would encounter these circumstances and situations, or what the intensity of them would be.

Sometimes the conflict can occur internally when a difference of opinion arises. An example of this occurs almost immediately when they are ready to begin their journey. In Acts 15:36-41, we read: "Sometime later Paul said to Barnabas: Let us go back and visit the brothers in all the towns where we preached the word of the Lord and see how they are doing. Barnabas wanted to take John, also called Mark, with them, but Paul did not think it wise to take him, because he had deserted them in Pamphylia and had not continued with them in the work. They had such a sharp disagreement that they parted company. Barnabas took Mark and sailed for Cyprus, but Paul chose Silas and left, commended by the brothers to the grace of the Lord. He went through Syria and Cilicia, strengthening the churches." The phrase to note is: "They had such a sharp disagreement that they parted company." A "sharp disagreement" conveys the sense of "a situation in which people express different opinions about something and sometimes argue." In this case with Barnabas and Paul, they chose not to travel together and each went his own way with the particular coworker of choice.

There is an interesting insight shared in Acts 20:17-27 (ASV) where Paul tells the Elders that which he is convinced of and feels compelled to do. We note these meaningful words: "And from Miletus he sent to Ephesus, and called to him the elders of the church. And when they were come to him, he said unto them, You yourselves know, from the first day that I set foot in Asia, after what manner I was with you all the time, serving the Lord with all lowliness of mind, and with tears, and with trials which befell me by the plots of the Jews; how I shrank not from declaring unto you anything that was profitable, and teaching you publicly, and from house to house, testifying both to Jews and to Greeks repentance toward God, and faith toward our Lord Jesus Christ. And now, behold, I go bound in the spirit unto Jerusalem, not knowing the things that shall befall me there: save that the Holy Spirit testifies unto me in every city, saying that bonds and afflictions abide me. But I hold not my life of any account as dear unto myself, so that I may accomplish my course, and the ministry which I received from the Lord Jesus, to testify the gospel of the grace of God. And now, behold, I know that ye all, among whom I went about preaching the kingdom, shall see my face no more. Wherefore I testify unto you this day, that I am pure from the blood of all men. For I shrank not from declaring unto you the whole counsel of God."

Another incident in the life of the Apostle Paul demonstrates his great determination and conviction to pour his entire body, soul and spirit into the accomplishment of the task given to him. He is persuaded that he needs to go to Rome and declare the Gospel there. Acts 27 is the account of his journey to Rome. Aboard the ship to Rome, there is a decision to be made whether to go on or to remain in port. Acts 27:10-12 (ASV expresses Paul's concern and the ultimate decision that was made: "Men, I can see that our voyage is going to be disastrous and bring great loss to ship and cargo, and to our own lives also. But the centurion, instead of listening to what Paul said, followed the advice of the pilot and of the owner of the ship. Since the harbor was unsuitable to winter in, the majority decided that we should sail on, hoping to reach Phoenix and winter there. This was a harbor in Crete, facing both southwest and northwest. One man, Paul, saw the possible peril if they continued on; but the majority prevailed that they should sail on." Was this a wise choice made by the majority? Acts 27:14-20 (ASV) supplies the answer: "Before very long, a wind of hurricane force, called the northeaster, swept down from the island. The ship was caught by the storm and could not head into the wind; so we gave way to it and were driven along. As we passed to the lee of a small island called Cauda, we were hardly able to make the lifeboat secure. When the men had hoisted it aboard, they passed ropes under the ship itself to hold it together. Fearing that they would run aground on the sandbars of Syrtis, they lowered the sea anchor and let the ship be driven along. We took such a violent battering from the storm that the next day they began to throw the cargo overboard. On the third day, they threw the ship's tackle overboard with their own hands. When neither sun nor stars appeared for many days and the storm continued raging, we finally gave up all hope of being saved."

What will the Lord do to get Paul to Rome so he can finish his race and ministry with joy? After days of uncertainty, Paul makes the following statement in Acts 27:21-26 (ASV), "After the men had gone a long time without food, Paul stood up before them and said: Men, you should have taken my advice not to sail from Crete; then you would have spared yourselves this damage and loss. But now I urge you to keep up your courage, because not one of you will be lost; only the ship will be destroyed. Last night an angel of the God whose I am and whom I serve stood beside me and said, Do not be afraid, Paul. You must stand trial before Caesar; and God has graciously given you the lives of all who sail with you. So keep up your courage, men, for I have faith in God that it will happen just as he told me. Nevertheless, we must run aground on some island." Is Paul in his right mind or is he hallucinating – seeing angels and hearing voices in the night? Why should seasoned seamen listen to a person who alleges he has been talking to an angel? What is Paul's plan – God's plan – to get the crew and Paul safely ashore?

Acts 27:33-44 (ASV) records the plan unfolding: "Just before dawn Paul urged them all to eat. For the last fourteen days, he said, you have been in constant suspense and have gone without food--you haven't eaten anything. Now I urge you to take some food. You need it to survive. Not one of you will lose a single hair from his head. After he said this, he took some bread and gave thanks to God in front of them all. Then he broke it and began to eat. They were all encouraged and ate some food themselves. Altogether there were 276 of us on board. When they had eaten as much as they wanted, they lightened the ship by throwing the grain into the sea. When daylight came, they did not recognize the land, but they saw a bay with a sandy beach, where they decided to run the ship aground if they could. Cutting loose the anchors, they left them in the sea and at the same time untied the ropes that held the rudders. Then they hoisted the foresail to the wind and made for the beach. But the ship struck a sandbar and ran aground. The bow stuck fast and would not move, and the stern was broken to pieces by the pounding of the surf. The soldiers planned to kill the prisoners to prevent any of them from swimming away and escaping. But the centurion wanted to spare Paul's life and kept them from carrying out their plan. He ordered those who could swim to jump overboard first and get to land. The rest were to get there on planks or on pieces of the ship. In this way everyone reached land in safety."

One can only wonder if we knew the lurking dangers that were awaiting us, would we continue on our journey. Would we be able to say that despite the unknowns and the high risk attached to going forward: "now I go bound in the spirit to Jerusalem, not knowing the things that will happen to me there, except that the Holy Spirit testifies in every city, saying that chains and tribulations await me"? Would we also echo the words: "to testify to the gospel of the grace of God?" In this regard, when was the most recent time when you were unafraid to face any potential risk as you served Christ and the Gospel?

Most of the time, the conflicts one experiences will be external when contrary individuals, religious organizations or the politically motivated purpose to thwart the message of the Gospel from being proclaimed. Paul, when confronting some false apostles, states some of the things he encountered and endured as he journeyed. The listing appears in II Corinthians 11:22-29, "Are they Hebrews? So am I. Are they Israelites? So am I. Are they the seed of Abraham? So am I. Are they ministers of Christ?--I speak as a fool--I am more: in labors more abundant, in stripes above measure, in prisons more frequently, in deaths often. From the Jews five times I received forty stripes minus one. Three times I was beaten with rods; once I was stoned; three times I was shipwrecked; a night and a day I have been in the deep; in journeys often, in perils of waters, in perils of robbers, in perils of my own countrymen, in perils of the Gentiles, in perils in the city, in perils in the wilderness, in perils in the sea, in perils among false brethren; in weariness and toil, in sleeplessness often, in hunger and thirst, in fastings often, in cold and nakedness--besides the other things, what comes upon me daily: my deep concern for all the churches. Who is weak, and I am not weak?"

When Paul set out on his mission to reach the world with the Gospel, he could not have predicted all of these various experiences he would encounter and have to endure. There are many who are known as "Christians" who have faced and are facing persecution (A classic tome regarding the historic persecution of believers is, *Foxe's Book of Martyrs* compiled by John

Foxe). From the historic to the present reports of persecution are numerous. A partial report by The Gatestone Institute reports: "The 2013 year began with reports indicating that wherever Christians live side by side with large numbers of Muslims, they are under attack. One report said that Africa, where Christianity spread fastest during the past century, now is the region where oppression of Christians is spreading fastest. This is certainly true: whether in Kenya, Nigeria, Mali, Somalia, Sudan, or Tanzania, attacks on Christians in those countries are as frequent as they are graphic. As for the Middle East, the cradle of Christianity, a new study by the Pew Forum finds that just 0.6 percent of the world's 2.2 billion Christians now live in the Middle East and North Africa. Christians make up only 4% of the region's inhabitants, drastically down from 20% a century ago and marking the smallest regional Christian minority in the world. Fully 93% of the region is Muslim, and 1.6% is Jewish. How Christianity became all but eradicated from the region where it was born is made clear by yet another report concerning Egypt's Christian Copts, the Middle East's largest Christian minority. Due to a climate of fear and uncertainty, Christian families are leaving Egypt in large numbers. Along with regular church attacks, the situation has gotten to the point that, according to one Coptic priest, Salafis meet Christian girls in the street and order them to cover their hair. Sometimes they hit them when they refuse. Another congregation leader said: With the new [Sharia-heavy] constitution, the new laws that are expected, and the majority in parliament I don't believe we can be treated on an equal basis. Elsewhere, Christians are not allowed to flee. In eastern Syria, for example, 25,000 Christians, including Syriac Orthodox, Syriac Catholics, Chaldeans and Armenians, were prevented from fleeing due to a number of roadblocks set up by armed Islamic militia groups, who deliberately target Christians for robbery and kidnapping for ransoming, often slaughtering their victims…"

The Washington Times reported on September 26, 2013, "Much of the focus on the tensions in the Middle East, Africa and Asia has been on which political group will ultimately gain power in the various struggles. However, the bombing of a church in Pakistan and the targeting of non-Muslims in the terrorist attack in Nairobi, Kenya highlight the vulnerability of religious minorities in many parts of the world. Sundays' attack on All Saint's Church, an Anglican church built in 1883 is the deadliest attack on Christians in Pakistan's history, killing 81 and injuring 140 church goers, according to the Associated Press. At the July 2013 briefing on religious freedom in Pakistan hosted by U.S. Commission on International Religious Freedom, Peter Bhatti said, "Christians feel insecure and fearful in their motherland. These (blasphemy) laws have encouraged hundreds of incidents during which innocent Christians have been victimized, persecuted, burnt alive, and had their churches and properties burnt and demolished. Many people currently are in prison and waiting for trials."

The U.S. State Department's International Religious Freedom Report for 2012 notes the global trend in religious freedoms has been negative. From authoritarian Communist countries like China and Cuba to Islamic nations like Saudi Arabia, 75% of the world's population lives in countries where there are severe restrictions on religion, according to Open Doors USA, an organization that tracks persecutions of Christians. A Pew Forum report on Global Christianity reported that Christians shrank from 9.5% of the population in the Middle East and North Africa in 1910 to only 3.8% of the population in 2010. Since 2010, the political turmoil and ascension of more militant Islamic governments has led to even more emigration of Christians from the region..."

The persecution pressures are impacting people throughout the world. Even in the United States of America, there are several instances where persecution is gradually becoming a reality. Most of the persecution pressures here and throughout the world are largely unreported or under-reported. The Washington Times article includes: "Egypt has the largest concentration of Christians in the Middle East, but tens of thousands of Copts have fled the country after President Mubarak's ouster according to human rights activists. There are daily reports of violence against the remaining Coptic populations. The Associated Press reported that Syrian Christians from the village of Maaloula were driven out or forcibly converted to Islam by rebels aligned with al-Qaida. That Christian community goes back to the birth of Christianity and still speaks Aramaic, the language of Jesus. Last year, a Public Broadcasting Service news report noted that the only Middle-Eastern country that has a growing Christian population is Israel. "There are no more Christians in Algeria, in Tunisia, in Libya, where there was a majority of Christians 700, 800 years ago. They're gone. There's not — there's no one," Mary-Jane Deeb, head of the Africa and Middle East division of the Library of Congress told PBS last year. "In the rest of the region that will also happen as more Christians are emigrating. They're leaving."

Jesus Christ spoke of events and persecutions that would take place as the end time approaches. In Mark 13:9-13 (NIV), Jesus said: "You must be on your guard. You will be handed over to the local councils and flogged in the synagogues. On account of me you will stand before governors and kings as witnesses to them. And the gospel must first be preached to all nations. Whenever you are arrested and brought to trial, do not worry beforehand about what to say. Just say whatever is given you at the time, for it is not you speaking, but the Holy Spirit. Brother will betray brother to death, and a father his child. Children will rebel against their parents and have them put to death. All men will hate you because of me, but he who stands firm to the end will be saved." These words address the collapse of both virtue and values in a culture that is drifting into chaos. Are we at that point in human history? Are we experiencing the disintegration of the family and a trend toward interpersonal relations within the home being abandoned? Are we seeing the acceleration of violence and a devaluing of life? Is there an increase of inhumanity being exhibited within our culture? Are people becoming weary of religious reference and influence in the ebb and flow of our culture? Is the church moving toward accommodation with the culture rather than maintaining an uncompromised posture before the world? Are we more given to the fear of man than we are of any genuine fear of God? Is the risk-factor too great for the average "Christian" to embrace and implement? Living "Amid The Cultural Chaos", is the "Christian" seen more as a casualty than a conqueror? If you would be assessed by the "great cloud of witnesses" mentioned in Hebrews 12:1 (looking back to those listed in Hebrews 11), how would you be identified – a casualty or a conqueror? Which one would you prefer to be – a casualty of a conqueror?

FOR THOUGHT AND REFLECTION:

If you were living in the day of Gideon (Judges 6 through 8), would you be numbered among the 29,700 who left the field of battle or with the 300 who were ready for battle?

Would you consider yourself as one who is continuing in the spiritual warfare or have you yielded to lesser things that are not as intense as the ongoing battle?

If a commentary was given about your life and commitment, would it include words similar to "exhausted but still in pursuit" and he/she "risked their lives for the name of our Lord Jesus Christ"? Why? Why not?

Do the words of a children's Hymn (Dare to be a Daniel): "Dare to have a purpose firm, Dare to make it known..." describe your purpose and commitment? In what ways is this true about you?

As an individual, would you have the courage to state to the majority who were of a different persuasion, Acts 27:25, "Therefore take heart (be of good courage)...for I believe God that it will be just as it was told me."?

But I do not account my life of any value
nor as precious to myself,
if only I may finish my course and the ministry
that I received from the Lord Jesus,
to testify to the gospel of the grace of God.
Acts 20:24 (ESV)

Now to him who is able to do far more abundantly
than all that we ask or think,
according to the power at work within us,
to him be glory in the church and in Christ Jesus
throughout all generations, forever and ever. Amen.
Ephesians 3:20-21 ESV)

9. Intimidation (Bullying)

The intimidation tactic has been employed for a very long time. It is not limited to one person to another person situation but includes nations as well. Since World War 1, the United States and the overwhelming number of nations signed an agreement that indicated that any use of Chemical Weapons is prohibited. For almost one-hundred years, most of the nations have upheld that agreement (only Germany in World War 2, Iraq, and Syria has been in violation of the agreement). The President of the United States indicated that the use of Chemical Weapons in the ongoing Civil War in Syria (2013) would be a game-changer. A term used by the President was that it would be a "red-line." The idea being conveyed is that the United States would take remedial action against the Syrian Government if they employed Chemical Weaponry against their own people or other nations. The warning was ignored and more than fourteen hundred Syrians were killed by the nerve gas Sarin. History will eventually record what occurred in this exchange of words regarding who did what and when it was done.

A similar exchange of words occurred in a Biblical context. As one looks back at biblical events and history, while the weaponry and strategy was different, the objective then was the same as any objective now. The basic idea is to impose one's will and objectives upon others with a superior force or weaponry being the intimidation tactic that brings about a desired result.

One of the miscalculations then and now is the God factor. Which God is being acknowledged and served? Which God exercises control over the world He created? While military strategists make a determination based upon troop and weapon strength, the religious persuasion in the contemporary world, the strength of one's faith, should also be understood as an important factor. One must believe there is a living God Who is in control of His universe at all times.

The more one is engaged in viable ministry for the Lord Jesus Christ, the more one will be exposed to opposition to both the message and the messenger. There is always the possibility of the Intimidation Factor being employed by a person or clique in a local church situation. Within the church, a "natural leader" will often emerge and be viewed by others as being their representative or spokesperson. It may be that the one perceived as being the primary "giver" that finances the local congregation should be the voice who addresses and tries to orchestrate the direction of the local ministry. This individual becomes the self-appointed arbitrator, agitator, or the determining voice for the church. An analysis of the attitude and actions of such a person could easily fit into a framework of intimidation (bullying). While some may not agree with this strong-willed individual, they are hesitant to be a voice of opposition lest it cause some form of repercussion or unrest (and an innate/latent fear of the bully-type).

There is an interesting illustration of an intimidation (bullying) approach referenced in II Kings 18-19 and Isaiah 37. The

King of Assyria has a design for the world of his day. It is his ambition and goal to bring all nations under his control and for them to be in subjugation to him and his decrees for them. It amounts to his being a dictator and the people being enslaved. To carry out his ambition and design, he has Sennacherib who is a very willing General to command king's army. When this army approaches Jerusalem, the troops number 185,000 men. This army is formidable and capable of overwhelming any nation at any time. Sennacherib is willing and able to demonstrate the authority of the King of Assyria and approaches his opposition with superiority, disdain, swagger and intimidation. Sennacherib's manner is that of a bully. His approach is the employment of fear-factors so that the people will choose not to offer any resistance.

The initial approach is mild at the outset. The challenge: "what confidence is this in which you trust?" One can see the subtlety of this approach in II Kings 18:17-24, "Then the king of Assyria sent...a great army against Jerusalem, to King Hezekiah. And they went up and came to Jerusalem...Say now to Hezekiah, Thus says the great king, the king of Assyria: What confidence is this in which you trust? You speak of having plans and power for war; but they are mere words. And in whom do you trust that you rebel against me? Now look! You are trusting in the staff of this broken reed, Egypt, on which if a man leans, it will go into his hand and pierce it. So is Pharaoh King of Egypt to all who trust in him. But if you say to me, we trust in the Lord our God, is it not He whose high places and whose altars Hezekiah has taken away, and said to Judah and Jerusalem, You shall worship before this altar in Jerusalem? Now therefore, I urge you, give a pledge to my master the king of Assyria, and I will give you two thousand horses--if you are able on your part to put riders on them! How then will you repel one captain of the least of my master's servants, and put your trust in Egypt for chariots and horsemen?"

The approach is one of deceptive enticement. The hope was that the people would be naïve or gullible and go along to get along. It's amazing how easily people can be enticed to compromise when the offer of things becomes a consideration rather than remaining committed to foundational principles, virtues and moral values. King Hezekiah had keen insight in terms of the strategies that might be employed to bring about capitulation and surrender. He had instructed the people not to respond to any challenge or any offer by the representatives of Assyria. The response and behavior of the people was commendable inasmuch as there is no verbal response to this subtle approach. For Sennacherib, it means that phase two of the Intimidation (bullying) will be introduced.

The accelerated intimidation is given in II Kings 18:28-35, "...Hear the word of the great king, the king of Assyria...Do not let Hezekiah deceive you, for he shall not be able to deliver you from his hand; nor let Hezekiah make you trust in the Lord, saying, The Lord will surely deliver us; this city shall not be given into the hand of the king of Assyria. Do not listen to Hezekiah; for thus says the king of Assyria: Make peace with me by a present and come out to me; and every one of you eat from his own vine and every one from his own fig tree, and every one of you drink the waters of his own cistern; until I come and take you away to a land like your own land, a land of grain and new wine, a land of bread and vineyards, a land of olive groves and honey, that you may live and not die. But do not listen to Hezekiah, lest he persuade you, saying, The Lord will deliver us. Has any of the gods of the nations at all delivered its land from the hand of the king of Assyria...Who among all the gods of the lands have delivered their countries from my hand, that the Lord should deliver Jerusalem from my hand?"

The words used now are not only intimidation, but they also reflect the disdain and disrespect of the Assyrians toward Israel and King Hezekiah, as well as rejection of The Lord. The phrases used are: (1) Do not let Hezekiah deceive you; (2) He shall not be able to deliver you; (3) Do not listen to Hezekiah, lest he persuade you, saying, The Lord will deliver us; (4) finally, he ridicules the name of The Lord. The approach of the Assyrian commander is to undermine the integrity of King Hezekiah and to convince the people that he is not a trustworthy leader. He points to other nations and their gods and asks: "who among all the gods of the lands have delivered countries from my hand?" The appeal of Sennacherib is: put your confidence in man and his superior military force. He wants the people to forget about Almighty God and the foundational principles, virtues and core values the people of God are to embrace and practice.

There is a sense where this event unfolding is similar to the Temptation of Jesus Christ recorded in Matthew 4:1-11. When the devil approaches Jesus Christ, what does he want to accomplish and/or thwart? The birth announcement of Jesus Christ stated His eternal purpose – "His name shall be called Jesus for He will save His people from their sin." The devil knows this eternal purpose but he is so prideful that it allows him to be undaunted in his approach to Jesus. The general area of Temptation is usually in terms of the lust of the flesh and eyes, and an appeal made to the pride of an individual. A summary of these areas is recorded in I John 2:15-17, "Do not love the world or the things in the world. If anyone loves the world, the love of the Father is not in him. For all that is in the world - the lust of the flesh, the lust of the eyes, and the pride of life is not of the Father but is of the world. And the world is passing away, and the lust of it; but he who does the will of God abides forever." This is the devil's approach to Jesus Christ and it continues to be his approach as he tries to tempt and divert one from the will and purpose of God. He failed in his effort to tempt and divert Jesus from His eternal mission. In like manner, as we follow the Lord Jesus Christ, we should refuse and refute the devil's efforts with us. Jesus cited the Word of God as He resisted the propositions and proposals of the devil. In like manner, we should know the Scripture and cite them as we resist the propositions and proposals of the devil to us. The instruction of Psalm 119:11 should be our commitment and practice, "Your word I have hidden (treasured) in my heart that I might not sin against You!"

It dovetails with the word of wisdom in Proverbs 4:23 "Keep your heart with all diligence, for out of it spring the issues of life." The New Living Translation renders this verse: "Above all else, guard your heart, for it affects everything you do."

Years ago, Dr. A.W. Tozer wrote a book entitled, *I Talk Back To The Devil: Essays In Spiritual Perfection*. His purpose was to be very practical in terms of God, His Word, and our application of it. He reminded his readers of an interesting perception: "Now, brethren, this is one of our greatest faults in our Christian lives. We are allowing too many rivals of God. We actually have too many gods. We have too many irons in the fire. We have too much theology that we don't understand. We have too much churchly institutionalism. We have too much religion." He includes two additional assessments: (1) "a very human habit of trusting in himself is generally the last great obstacle blocking his pathway to victory in Christian experience." (2) "Every grace and every virtue proceeds from God alone, and that not even a good thought can come from us except it be of Him." What is the point being made here? Dr. Tozer knew the dangers of a spiritual egoism. It is a subtlety of a New Age Philosophy which allows one to have a vision of personal grandeur and superiority to other people and any temporal situation one might encounter. It is self-confidence taken to an ultimate extreme. The Apostle Paul was cognizant of this danger when he reminded the Corinthian Church of their history. In I Corinthians 10, he begins with a review of the Children of Israel departing Egypt and traveling through the wilderness. He reminds them of the lessons they should learn from this history. Then, in I Corinthians 10:12, there is the cautionary word regarding self-confidence, new age philosophy, and spiritual egoism: "Therefore let him who thinks he stands take heed lest he fall." There is also the reminder to the follower of Christ to remain steadfast upon the firm foundation of God's Word and maintaining the core values and standards they contain. In Hebrews 2:1, the word is: "Therefore we must give the more earnest heed to the things we have heard, lest we drift away." These two verses – I Corinthians 10:12 and Hebrews 2:1 – are connected. There is considerable danger in allowing a spiritual egoism to become the self-confidence one embraces. This type of spiritual egoism will gradually drift into an unwarranted spiritual superiority over others. It can have a negative result in others and will surely be a detriment of the one succumbing to a spiritual egoism lifestyle.

How should one respond to the attacks and confrontations of our enemy? When he engages intimidation and ridicule, should it be ignored? How should one respond to intimidation and ridicule? A normal reaction is to "fight fire with fire" and to respond in kind. Should one become engaged in confrontation and try to counteract the intimidation (bullying) with argument or rash declarations? We are given the sense of how Hezekiah and the people will respond to Sennacherib in II Kings 19:1-7.

There are at least three things that Hezekiah does when he hears the words of Sennacherib. First, "when King Hezekiah heard this, he tore his clothes and put on sackcloth and went into the temple of the Lord. Second, he sent Eliakim the palace administrator, Shebna the secretary and the leading priests, all wearing sack-cloth, to the prophet Isaiah son of Amoz. They told him, "This is what Hezekiah says: This day is a day of distress and rebuke and disgrace, as when children come to the point of birth and there is no strength to deliver them. It may be that the Lord your God will hear all the words of the field commander, whom his master, the king of Assyria, has sent to ridicule the living God, and that he will rebuke him for the words the Lord your God has heard." Isaiah does not consider this as a trivial matter and is quick to reply to the pressing issue being faced by King Hezekiah and the people of God. The response is terse: "...Isaiah said to them, Tell your master, this is what the Lord says: Do not be afraid of what you have heard - those words with which the underlings of the king of Assyria have blasphemed me. Listen! I am going to put such a spirit in him that when he hears a certain report, he will return to his own country, and there I will have him cut down with the sword." Sennacherib and the King of Assyria were guilty of a miscalculation often embraced by people. Their error is that they fail to recognize and reckon with an Eternal God Who created this universe and sustains it by His will and power. They have not considered that only He will decree what will happen. The King of Assyria and Sennacherib needed to learn the lesson of Proverbs 21:1, "The king's heart is in the hand of the Lord, like the rivers of water; He turns it wherever He wishes." They needed to understand the source of confidence that David shared in Psalm 20:6-7, "Now I know that the Lord saves His anointed; He will answer him from His holy heaven with the saving strength of His right hand. Some trust in chariots, and some in horses; but we will remember the name of the Lord our God." The secular-oriented person can never appreciate or accept the reality that God plus one is a majority. Sennacherib will learn this – but – it will be too late and it will cost him his life.

The third thing King Hezekiah does is to come before the Lord – alone – in earnest prayer. We have a very beautiful picture and instruction regarding how one may (should) approach God in prayer. In II Kings 19:14-19, the picture is of one who is not only earnest regarding prayer but is equally intense. The text states: "Then he went up to the temple of the Lord and spread it out before the Lord. And Hezekiah prayed to the Lord: O Lord, God of Israel, enthroned between the cherubim, you alone are God over all the kingdoms of the earth. You have made heaven and earth. Give ear, O Lord, and hear; open your eyes, O Lord, and see; listen to the words Sennacherib has sent to insult the living God. It is true, O Lord, that the Assyrian kings have laid waste these nations and their lands. They have thrown their gods into the fire and destroyed them, for they were not gods but only wood and stone, fashioned by men's hands. Now, O Lord our God, deliver us from his hand, so that all kingdoms on earth may know that you alone, O Lord, are God."

The obvious is stated in regard to those whose gods were the working of men's hands and lacking any power or credibility in terms of comparison with The Creator and Eternal God. The prayer is not only a request but also worship of The Living God.

We would do well to remember this as and when we come before the Lord in prayer. Will this prayer be effectual? Will it bring about the desired result? In terms of effective/effectual prayer, the instruction in James 5:16 is: "Confess your trespasses to one another, and pray for one another, that you may be healed. The effective, fervent prayer of a righteous man avails much." Is this your approach as you come before God in prayer? J. B. Philipps renders this text: "You should get into the habit of admitting your sins to each other, and praying for each other, so that if sickness comes to you, you may be healed. Tremendous power is made available through a good man's earnest prayer." How often has this approach to prayer been practiced in your personal life or "church"? Do we have a deep-rooted belief that this is both valid and necessary as one comes before God?

In his headiness, Sennacherib believed his intimidation (bullying) approach would be effective with Hezekiah and the people of God. He also believed that his ridicule of and disdain for the Eternal God would suppress any appeal to Him or action by Him. In that regard, he may have thought he could intimidate God – if there was a God. He did not allow that any of his taunts or tactics would ultimately be gross miscalculations. There is a bigger picture than that drawn by Sennacherib. The people of God need to remind themselves of Who God is and what God is able to do. Does God hear this earnest and intense plea for help? Yes! Will God respond to this desperate plea for help and action? Yes! More importantly, will God make a statement regarding Who He is as He delivers His people from their enemy? Yes!

God's answer should remind us of the reality and possibilities of Ephesians 3:20-21, "Now to Him who is able to do exceedingly abundantly above all that we ask or think, according to the power that works in us, to Him be glory in the church by Christ Jesus to all generations, forever and ever. Amen". Too often, we may actually place our limitations onto the unlimited God. We may actually pray in terms of personal strength rather than on the omnipotence (unlimited power) of Almighty God.

The response of God is given in II Kings 19:32-37 (ASV), "Therefore thus says Jehovah concerning the king of Assyria, He shall not come unto this city, nor shoot an arrow there, neither shall he come before it with shield, nor cast up a mound against it. By the way that he came, by the same shall he return, and he shall not come unto this city, says Jehovah. For I will defend this city to save it, for mine own sake, and for my servant David's sake. And it came to pass that night that the angel of Jehovah went forth, and smote in the camp of the Assyrians - 185,000 - and when men arose early in the morning, behold, these were all dead bodies. So Sennacherib king of Assyria departed, and went and returned, and dwelt at Nineveh." Who would have expected this possibility becoming a reality? The NIV translates Ephesians 3:20, "Now to him who is able to do immeasurably more than all we ask or imagine, according to his power that is at work within us." Who would have asked or imagined that during one night 185,000 soldiers in Sennacherib's army would be struck down by an angel of God? Sennacherib had an instant wake-up call. All of his swagger, denunciation, intimidating (bullying) remarks, and disdain for Almighty God had been brought to a complete stop. What can Sennacherib do? II Kings 19 continues, "So Sennacherib king of Assyria broke camp and withdrew. He returned to Nineveh and stayed there. One day, while he was worshiping in the temple of his god Nisroch, his sons...cut him down with the sword, and they escaped to the land of Ararat."

Does God know the plight of His people? Yes! Does God hear their plea and prayer? Yes! Will God respond promptly to the desperate need and situation confronting His people? Yes! Will God make Himself known among the nations of men who have rejected Him? Yes! Will those who have rejected Him be brought to the place of acknowledgement that He alone is God, The Lord? Yes! Is God able to work similarly in the twenty-first century if His people seek Him on His terms? Yes!

Isaiah goes on to state a great truth about The Only True God. In Isaiah 45:22-24, "Look to Me, and be saved, all you ends of the earth! For I am God, and there is no other. I have sworn by Myself; the word has gone out of My mouth in righteousness, and shall not return, that to Me every knee shall bow, every tongue shall take an oath. He shall say, surely in the Lord I have righteousness and strength. To Him men shall come." These words are repeated in Romans 14:7-12. The thrust of the words are that all men will have to face the eternal God. Paul emphasizes this truth when he writes: "For none of us lives to himself, and no one dies to himself. For if we live, we live to the Lord; and if we die, we die to the Lord. Therefore, whether we live or die, we are the Lord's. For to this end Christ died and rose and lived again, that He might be Lord of both the dead and the living. But why do you judge your brother? Or why do you show contempt for your brother? For we shall all stand before the judgment seat of Christ. For it is written: As I live, says the Lord, every knee shall bow to Me, and every tongue shall confess to God. So then each of us shall give account of himself to God…"

It is interesting to observe how God frustrates the will and plans of mankind. We need to remind ourselves of who we are in Christ and where we are positionally. The words of I Corinthians 1:18-19 should be an encouragement: "For the message of the cross is foolishness to those who are perishing, but to us who are being saved it is the power of God. For it is written: I will destroy the wisdom of the wise, and bring to nothing the understanding of the prudent." The point being made is that God is in control of all things and provides a refuge for His people at all times. He also wants His people to appreciate the relationship He has established with them. He wants to see a greater degree of commitment by His people as they follow Him and respond to Him wholeheartedly.

There is this interesting paragraph by C.S. Lewis in *Mere Christianity*. He writes: "Give me all of you!!! I don't want so much of your time, so much of your talents and money, and so much of your work. I want YOU!!! ALL OF YOU!! I have not come to torment or frustrate the natural man or woman, but to KILL IT! No half measures will do. I don't want to only prune a branch here and a branch there; rather I want the whole tree out! Hand it over to me, the whole outfit, all of your desires, all of your wants and wishes and dreams. Turn them ALL over to me, give yourself to me and I will make of you a new self—in my image. Give me yourself and in exchange I will give you Myself. My will shall become your will. My heart shall become your heart." C.S. Lewis is attempting to convey that greater commitment and loyalty must be evidenced in a person's life in Christ. All things does not equate with some things.

If this becomes one's relationship with Christ and daily walk with the Lord, then those who would seek to cause one harm by means of confrontations, ridicule, intimidation (bullying) or threat will be frustrated by the Lord we are committed to honor and serve. It would be well to exercise the practice of Hezekiah in prayer, namely, spreading it all out before the Lord.

FOR THOUGHT AND REFLECTION:

In your decision-making process, what are some of the key things you consider and utilize as a priority?

At times when you are challenged by 'group-think' (a form of peer pressure), do you allow that to (a) influence or (b) intimidate you? Are you easily bullied? Explain your response.

If in the providence of God, we were living in an enemy-occupied area, how would you practice your faith/religion? Some ancillary questions to include in your response: (1) would you attend a secret prayer and Bible Study Group? (2) Would you host one in your home? (3) What would you do with your Bible?

If we were at a point in our lives similar to German believers during World War II, and we were hiding believers in our home, how would you answer an enemy inquiry in this regard? Would you (a) tell the truth, or (b) frame a response that would evade a direct answer?

If someone attempted to (a) intimidate (bully) you and (b) mock and deride the Lord your God, what are the first things you would do (or not do)? Would you be motivated by Psalm 118:4-8?

"Let them now that fear Jehovah say,
That his loving-kindness [endures] forever.
Out of my distress I called upon Jehovah:
Jehovah answered me [and set me] in a large place.
Jehovah is on my side; I will not fear: What can man do unto me?
Jehovah is on my side among them that help me:
Therefore shall I see [my desire] upon them that hate me.
It is better to take refuge in Jehovah than to put confidence in man.
Psalm 118:4-8 (ASV)

May we all be found faithful and zealous as we take our place in and "Amid The Cultural Chaos" and do what our Great Commander declares. As and when we do, that will lead us on to Victory and Conquering in His Name (I Corinthians 15:57). "Amid The Cultural Chaos" of the day, don't permit yourself to become A Casualty, rather be A Conqueror in/through Jesus Christ. The words of Romans 8:37 should resonate in our heart, soul and mind at all times, "Yet in all these things we are more than conquerors through Him who loved us."

10. Being Factual or Fallacious

In one of his early writings, *Escape From Reason* (1968), Dr. Francis A. Schaeffer summarized his basic thesis with these words (Chapter 2): "It is an important principle to remember, in the contemporary interest in communication and in language study, that the Biblical presentation is that though we do not have exhaustive truth, we have from the Bible what I term true truth. In this way we know the true truth about God, true truth about man, and something truly about nature. Thus on the basis of the Scriptures, while we do not have exhaustive knowledge, we have true and unified knowledge." The question then and now is similar - is truth in jeopardy today? Is integrity being compromised? Has honesty departed as a viable part of our culture and lives? Why is there a loss of believability? What has happened to an ethical and moral lifestyle and commitment? When did "a man's word is his bond" become lost in human interaction? Is it far-fetched to expect honesty in human discourse and interaction?

Dr. Schaeffer was aware of the foibles of mankind and the tremendous influence of the culture upon one's thinking and ultimate actions. He saw these as departures from truth, human dignity and rational thought. A reason for his publishing his observations was his concern for the cultural slide that had begun (Chapter 3): "We are watching our culture put into effect the fact that when you tell men long enough that they are machines, it soon begins to show in their actions. You see it in our whole culture – in the theatre of cruelty, in the violence in the streets, in the death of man in art and life."

The Apostle Paul emphasized the necessity for the presence of truth in one's life and relationships. As he wrote his letter to the Church in Ephesus, he set out to establish the foundation upon which one must stand. Ephesians 4:11-13 (NIV) states this focus and concern: "It was he who gave some to be apostles, some to be prophets, some to be evangelists, and some to be pastors and teachers, to prepare God's people for works of service, so that the body of Christ may be built up until we all reach unity in the faith and in the knowledge of the Son of God and become mature, attaining to the whole measure of the fullness of Christ." The basic way by which this would occur is the presence and place of truth in one's life and in all relationships. In Ephesians 4:15, 25 (NIV), he writes: " Instead, speaking the truth in love, we will in all things grow up into him who is the Head, that is, Christ...Therefore each of you must put off falsehood and speak truthfully to his neighbor, for we are all members of one body." Paul does not want the people in the church to get ensnared by the cultural slide that was occurring. His rationale for the emphasis upon truth is given in Ephesians 4:17-24 (NIV), "So I tell you this, and insist on it in the Lord, that you must no longer live as the Gentiles do, in the futility of their thinking. They are darkened in their understanding and separated from the life of God because of the ignorance that is in them due to the hardening of their hearts. Having lost all sensitivity, they have given themselves over to sensuality so as to indulge in every kind of impurity, with a continual lust for more. You, however, did not come to know Christ that way. Surely you heard of him and were taught in him in accordance with the truth that is in Jesus. You were taught, with regard to your former way of life, to put off your old self, which is being corrupted by its deceitful desires; to be made new in the attitude of your minds; and to put on the new self, created to be like God in true righteousness and holiness." These standards for faith and practice are applicable for all generations. It is of considerable importance in terms of whether one lives as a "Cultural Casualty" or as a "Cultural Conqueror." Additionally, if edification within the body of Christ (The Church) is to occur, it will be based upon truth and transparency. If integrity is waning or lacking, there is a character issue that must be addressed. If honesty is absent in ones interaction with others, there is a relational issue that must be addressed.

Paul emphasizes one additional point in terms of truth and integrity in verse 29: "Let no corrupt word proceed out of your mouth, but what is good for necessary edification, that It may impart grace to the hearers." The "corrupt word" is in the area of deceit, verbal fraud, hypocrisy, unrighteous thoughts and words, lack of truthfulness or honesty, perpetrating of a hoax or hoaxes, and all other kinds of verbal or written misrepresentations. When the moral compass has been jettisoned, there are no boundaries restricting the actions and interactions of the human race. The Word of the Lord is clear and precise in this regard. In Jeremiah 17:5-10 (selected), "Thus says the Lord: Cursed is the man who trusts in man and makes flesh his strength, whose heart departs from the Lord...The heart is deceitful above all things, And desperately wicked; Who can know it? I, the Lord, search the heart, I test the mind, even to give every man according to his ways, according to the fruit of his doings." Truth will be part of the measurement God employs regarding one's life. He sees and knows every detail of one's life all of the time. He knows every word that is spoken and for which all will give an account. A precursor to the flood is stated in Genesis 6:5-7, "Then the Lord saw that the wickedness of man was great in the earth, and that every intent of the thoughts of his heart was only evil continually. And the Lord was sorry that He had made man on the earth, and He was grieved in His heart. So the Lord said, I will destroy man whom I have created from the face of the earth, both man and beast, creeping thing and birds of the air, for I am sorry that I have made them." It was a departure from and a jettisoning of integrity/truth that contributed greatly to the decline of virtue and moral values prior to the flood. The people of Noah's day neglected and ignored the fact that God knows all and makes His determinations based upon His infallible knowledge. He is measuring all people and nations by His absolute standard of truth, righteousness and holiness.

Further along in history, the Prophet Isaiah wrote and prophesied about the cultural erosion and slide in his day. Once again, the issue is falsehood versus truth. His words in Isaiah

59:1-15 (ASV - Selected) indicate how far the cultural slide had taken the people of his day: "Behold, Jehovah's hand is not shortened, that it cannot save; neither his ear heavy, that it cannot hear: but your iniquities have separated between you and your God, and your sins have hid his face from you, so that he will not hear. For your hands are defiled with blood, and your fingers with iniquity; your lips have spoken lies, your tongue mutters wickedness. None sues in righteousness, and none pleads in truth: they trust in vanity, and speak lies; they conceive mischief, and bring forth iniquity...their works are works of iniquity, and the act of violence is in their hands. Their feet run to evil, and they make haste to shed innocent blood: their thoughts are thoughts of iniquity; desolation and destruction are in their paths. The way of peace they know not; and there is no justice in their goings: they have made them crooked paths; whosoever goes therein does not know peace. Therefore justice is far from us, neither does righteousness overtake us: we look for light, but, behold, darkness; for brightness, but we walk in obscurity. We grope for the wall like the blind; we grope as they that have no eyes: we stumble at noonday as in the twilight; among them that are lusty we are as dead men...we look for justice, but there is none; for salvation, but it is far off from us. For our transgressions are multiplied before You, and our sins testify against us; for our transgressions are with us, and as for our iniquities, we know them: transgressing and denying Jehovah, and turning away from following our God, speaking oppression and revolt, conceiving and uttering from the heart words of falsehood. And justice is turned away backward, and righteousness stands afar off; for truth is fallen in the street, and uprightness cannot enter…truth is lacking; and he that departs from evil makes himself a prey. And Jehovah saw it, and it displeased him that there was no justice."

The emphasis is upon the reality that the human race is caught in the cultural slide and an accelerating momentum is occurring. If we compare the culture of our day with that indicated in the day of both Isaiah and Paul, we find parallels and similarity. We must pause and ask ourselves: (1) are there roadblocks today that are limiting Christian effectiveness, and (2) are there roadblocks limiting Christian living and service? If so, what are some of these roadblocks and why have they been allowed to occur? Is the downward momentum of our day so great that it cannot be reversed?

An alternate reading of Isaiah 59:12-16 (NLT) sounds equally overwhelming: "For our sins are piled up before God and testify against us. Yes, we know what sinners we are. We know that we have rebelled against the Lord. We have turned our backs on God. We know how unfair and oppressive we have been, carefully planning our deceitful lies. Our courts oppose people who are righteous, and justice is nowhere to be found. Truth falls dead in the streets, and fairness has been outlawed. Yes, truth is gone, and anyone who tries to live a godly life is soon attacked. The Lord looked and was displeased to find that there was no justice. He was amazed to see that no one intervened to help the oppressed. So He Himself stepped in to save them with his mighty power and justice..." Are these words descriptive of these times in which we are living? The Word of the Lord needs to be applied currently because the only way to halt the cultural slide is by and through the intervention of the Lord. We do not know when He will intervene – all we know is that He will step in at the appropriate moment within His plan and purpose for His universe.

When we consider some of the roadblocks that interrupt and/or interfere with the level of Christian effectiveness, as well as impacting the Christian's living and service, we find that the loss of integrity is a significant reason for the decline. In a recent Blog, I wrote and raised a question: "Have members of the clergy become lazy to the point where they copy someone else's work product and represent it as being their own?" Has plagiarism become a norm within the "church"? If there are men who stand before congregations doing this, what prevents this from being identified as copyright infringement or the perpetration of a fraud? Whether it is sermon content or making reprints of copyrighted music, how has this been allowed to happen when truth, righteousness and holiness is the standard that should be embraced? Has the "church" been lulled to the point where the convenient is more preferable than conviction/commitment? If plagiarism and/or copyright infringement is occurring without any attribution or conviction, this is a lack of integrity. The fact is that both fraudulence and lack of integrity is taking place in the "church" and with some clergy.

Some time ago in a post on Facebook, Edgar Andrews made an excellent and earnest plea for attribution: "May I make a plea for those posting quotations (especially obscure ones) to include the source of any quotation and a full reference wherever possible? Others cannot make use of your insights unless they know where these insights are coming from, so posts without references are largely wasted!" As I thought and reflected about this post, I came to a conclusion: "…it is possible to cross a line and compromise one's integrity in such matters - maybe to the point of Isaiah 59:14 (The Message Paraphrase) becoming the assessment or observation of one's efforts - "Truth staggers down the street, Honesty is nowhere to be found…"

The clergy needs to remember a basic part of their calling. In II Timothy 2:15-17, "Be diligent to present yourself approved to God, a worker who does not need to be ashamed, rightly dividing the word of truth. But shun profane and idle babblings, for they will increase to more ungodliness. And their message will spread like cancer…" The direction to Timothy (and us) is clear and obvious. The component elements are (a) study; (b) be approved unto God, (c) never allow anything that will result in the need to be ashamed, (d) rightly study the Word of God, (e) exegete and proclaim the Word of Truth, applying and incorporating in all areas of one's life (f) be diligent.

The foundational principle for the Clergy is the focus of Jesus Christ and that which He would have His servants embrace. Integrity/truthfulness is basic to one's existence as a godly Clergyman. It is by example and instruction that a person, church and community will be impacted by and with God's truth. John 8:30-32 reminds one of the viewpoint and requirement of Jesus Christ: "As He (Jesus) spoke these words, many believed in Him. Then Jesus said to those Jews who believed Him, If you abide in My word, you are My disciples indeed. And you shall know the truth, and the truth shall make you free." In terms of the truth, Jesus also said in John 14:6, 12-15. "...I am the way, the truth, and the life. No one comes to the Father except through Me...Most assuredly, I say to you, he who believes in Me, the works that I do he will do also; and greater works than these he will do, because I go to My Father. And whatever you ask in My name, that I will do, that the Father may be glorified in the Son. If you ask anything in My name, I will do it. If you love Me, keep My commandments." Truth must dominate one's thinking and character. His truth must govern one's thoughts, words and deeds.

There is another side to Truth being the standard by which all else is measured. One place to consider is I John 1:6-10 (especially verses 6, 8, 10), "If we say that we have fellowship with Him, and walk in darkness, we lie and do not practice the truth...If we say that we have no sin, we deceive ourselves, and the truth is not in us...If we say that we have not sinned, we make Him a liar, and His word is not in us..." The phrase that begins each verse - "if we say" - makes this matter very personal. Dr. Adrian Rogers has a very succinct sermon outline on this text. His points are headed by "The Evolution of a Lie": "We Lie To

Deny Sin" (V.6); "We Lie To Deceive Ourselves and Others" (V.8), and "We Lie to Defy The Savior" (V.10).

Truth as a foundational principle and Integrity as a Character Trait are essential. It begins with one's relationship with Christ and extends out as others see and hear truth emanating from the child and servant of God. Questions that need to be reviewed and responded to frequently are: How well am I living day by day? How well do I examine my personal life by comparing it with the Word of God and what it requires of me? Do I realize that being good and doing good does not equate with the need for repentance of my sin? Do I acknowledge that in some thought, word, deed or attitude, I have sinned and fallen short of the glory of God? Do I realize the significance of my life being lived in conformity to the word of God? Do I remind myself that the primary goal of my life is to glorify God in all things and at all times?

Part of the consideration of one being either factual or fallacious pertains to one's own personal view of and commitment to integrity. We would be well-served by personally asking and answering additional questions: (1) What is the most fair and objective way to determine the level of one's integrity today? (2) In the affairs of Government, Education, Family Life and The Church, what is the consensus regarding integrity? (3) In personal matters – one's own business transactions – is integrity sometimes and/or conveniently compromised? The bottom line for all of us is: Are we taking a serious God seriously, and are we taking the Word of God (the Holy Scriptures) seriously?

I posted a Blog entitled "Fraudulence" in August 2013 where I commented: "My wife and I have found it both interesting and intriguing to watch some of the court programs on television. Two of them close to our Lunch Hour are The People's Court and Judge Alex. Part of our interest is in two aspects of several cases: (a) the naiveté and gullibility factors, and (b) the deceptions, lies and fraudulent statements made by individuals who have sworn to tell the truth. Why is it that some people have no compunction (a feeling of uneasiness or anxiety of the conscience caused by regret for doing wrong or causing pain; contrition; remorse) when giving testimony they know is fraudulent? When one gives fraudulent testimony, it is "acting with or having the intent to deceive." The World Dictionary allows that related words are: "duplicity, deceit…hoax." The bottom line to all of this is that there is clearly a deficit in one's character when fraudulent statements are made and devious actions are taken."

I also shared an observation on an event that occurred. On August 28th, 2013 it "…represented the 50th anniversary of the infamous march on Washington, DC. Equally infamous is the speech given by Martin Luther King, Jr. and the line that has often been repeated but not always exercised. He referenced his children and the hope that one day they would not be measured by the color of their skin but by the content of their character. It is the phrase – "the content of their character" – that should receive greater emphasis and exercise in the current trend of our time." In terms of "the content of one's character", where does one go to find a starting point for and a measurement of purposeful character content? Where does one begin to both know and assess what one's character is intended to be?

One place and possibility is II Peter 1:3-11 (ASV). It allows us to determine whether or not one's life is authentic before God. It also allows one to assess whether or not one is modeling fact or fallacy in daily living. The passage states: "...seeing that his divine power hath granted unto us all things that pertain unto life and godliness, through the knowledge of him that called us by his own glory and virtue; whereby he hath granted unto us his precious and exceeding great promises; that through these you may become partakers of the divine nature, having escaped from the corruption that is in that world by lust. Yes, and for this very cause adding on your part all diligence, in your faith supply virtue; and in your virtue knowledge; and in your knowledge self-control; and in your self-control patience; and in your patience godliness; and in your godliness brotherly kindness; and in your brotherly kindness love. For if these things are yours and abound, they make you to be neither idle nor unfruitful unto the knowledge of our Lord Jesus Christ. For he that lacks these things is blind, seeing only what is near, having forgotten the cleansing from his old sins. Wherefore, brethren, give the more diligence to make your calling and election sure: for if you do these things, you shall never stumble: for thus shall be richly supplied unto you the entrance into the eternal kingdom of our Lord and Savior Jesus Christ..." The first area mentioned as the priority to be added to one's faith is virtue. As one lives *Amid The Cultural Chaos*, both faith and virtue are absent in the thinking and practice among people. When that occurs, one has become "A Casualty" rather than "A Conqueror."

The intriguing part of these verses in terms of the content of one's character is the phrase of verse 4, "...through these you may be partakers of the divine nature..." To have the correct content of character one must have the correct commitment to Jesus Christ. The remainder of verse 4 addresses how one can cope and survive amid the cultural slide, namely, "...having escaped the corruption that is in the world through lust..." It is all part of possessing the divine nature and having a consecrated character before the Holy God. The other part of correct content of character is that it is based upon "...by which have been given to us exceedingly great and precious promises..." Standing upon the promises of God is a wise choice and experience.

The Character Traits one should develop and pursue are given in verses 5-7, "...giving all diligence, add to your faith virtue, to virtue knowledge, to knowledge self-control, to self-control perseverance, to perseverance godliness, to godliness brotherly kindness, and to brotherly kindness love." These are minimal goals for the child of God. However, even at this juncture in one's spiritual maturity process, there is a tremendous assurance given us in Verse 8, 10: "...For if these things are yours and abound, you will be neither barren nor unfruitful in the knowledge of our Lord Jesus Christ...be even more diligent to make your call and election sure, for if you do these things you will never stumble..." What a joy to know that, if these things are the fiber of our faith and practice, they will keep us from being ineffective and unproductive. In like manner, if we are doing these things, we will never fall. In this regard: (1) How well are you doing with God's character traits for you? (2) How close are you to participating in the divine nature? (3) Do you possess these qualities in increasing measure? (4) How effective is your influence in the world and culture in the 21st century? Are you having an effect? Are you making progress?

My blog continued: "In an article appearing in World Magazine on July 27th, 2013 – "Going Pagan" by Thomas Kidd, he wrote: "Evidence continues to mount that Christianity in Britain—and even belief in God's Existence—is on its way toward minority status. In a recent...poll of British young adults, only 25 percent unequivocally affirmed a belief in God, and 38 percent said they did not believe in God or any greater spiritual power. Meanwhile, one of the Church of England's recent proposals for attracting the young and un-churched is creating a pagan church with Christian content. Recent census data revealed that pagans were the 7th largest religious group in the United Kingdom, and that the number of pagans doubled between 2001 and 2011. (Atheists have worked to get Britons to stop identifying as Christians on the census, and even larger numbers label themselves "Jedi Knights" than pagans.) A summer solstice gathering... highlights the British pagan spiritual calendar..."

Could this be what America is in the process of becoming? Why is the "church" so marginalized in the world today? Why is the culture, world and our nation ignoring the truth? What has caused the gradual decline that has led to the slippery slope of today? Some biblical thoughts and ideas regarding the decline and marginalization include Jeremiah 23:11-13, "For both prophet and priest are profane; yes, in My house I have found their wickedness, says the Lord. Therefore their way shall be to them like slippery ways; in the darkness they shall be driven on and fall in them; for I will bring disaster on them, the year of their punishment, says the Lord. And I have seen folly in the prophets of Samaria: They prophesied by Baal and caused My people Israel to err..." The New Living Translation renders this text: Now for what God says regarding the lying prophets: "Can you believe it? A country teeming with adulterers! Faithless, promiscuous idolater-adulterers! They're a curse on the land. The land's a wasteland. Their unfaithfulness is turning the country into a cesspool, prophets and priests devoted to desecration. They have nothing to do with me as their God. My very own Temple, mind you - mud-spattered with their crimes. But they won't get by with it. They'll find themselves on a slippery slope, careening into the darkness, somersaulting into the pitch-black dark. I'll make them pay for their crimes. It will be the Year of Doom. Over in Samaria I saw prophets acting like silly fools - shocking! They preached using that no-god Baal for a text, messing with the minds of my people..." Where are we as a culture, nation, and church? Where are we supposed to be as a Child of God? Have we become afraid and weary of the struggle and life in the arena?

  We should be encouraged, motivated and challenged by the words contained in "The Man In The Arena" (An Excerpt

Taken From the Speech: "Citizenship In A Republic" A 35 Page speech by Theodore Roosevelt – given in Paris, France – April 23, 1910): "It is not the critic who counts; not the man who points out how the strong man stumbles, or where the doer of deeds could have done them better. The credit belongs to the man who is actually in the arena, whose face is marred by dust and sweat and blood; who strives valiantly; who errs, who comes short again and again, because there is no effort without error and shortcoming; but who does actually strive to do the deeds; who knows great enthusiasms, the great devotions; who spends himself in a worthy cause; who at the best knows in the end the triumph of high achievement, and who at the worst, if he fails, at least fails while daring greatly, so that his place shall never be with those cold and timid souls who neither know victory nor defeat."

There will be several pressures and perils – In The Arena… The Psalmist cried out to God for help and mercy as he tried to survive life in the arena. He shares his concerns in Psalm 94:14-23 (ASV), "For Jehovah will not cast off his people, neither will he forsake his inheritance. For judgment shall return unto righteousness; and all the upright in heart shall follow it. Who will rise up for me against the evil-doers? Who will stand up for me against the workers of iniquity? Unless Jehovah had been my help, my soul had soon dwelt in silence. When I said, my foot slips; Thy loving-kindness, O Jehovah, held me up. In the multitude of my thoughts within me Thy comforts delight my soul. Shall the throne of wickedness have fellowship with You, who frames mischief by statute? They gather themselves together against the soul of the righteous, and condemn the innocent blood. But Jehovah hath been my high tower, and my God the rock of my refuge. And he hath brought upon them their own iniquity, and will cut them off in their own wickedness; Jehovah our God will cut them off."

The previous referenced Blog closed with these references and citations. To a nation in another day, the Lord spoke through His prophet, Jeremiah 9:3-10, and said: "...like their bow they have bent their tongues for lies. They are not valiant for the truth on the earth. For they proceed from evil to evil, and they do not know Me...Everyone will deceive his neighbor, and will not speak the truth; they have taught their tongue to speak lies; they weary themselves to commit iniquity...Through deceit they refuse to know Me, says the Lord...Their tongue is an arrow shot out; it speaks deceit; one speaks peaceably to his neighbor with his mouth, but in his heart he lies in wait. Shall I not punish them for these things, says the Lord? Shall I not avenge Myself on such a nation as this?" Obviously, integrity has been sacrificed; deception has been embraced, and character is being destroyed. This question is then asked by the Lord: "Should I not punish them for this, declares the Lord? Should I not avenge myself on such a nation as this?" Is God being unjust when He makes this assessment and declaration?

Consider The Lord's statements and rationale in Isaiah 59:4, 14-15, "No one calls for justice, nor does any plead for truth. They trust in empty words and speak lies; they conceive evil and bring forth iniquity...Justice is turned back, and righteousness stands afar off; for truth is fallen in the street, and equity cannot enter. So truth fails, and he who departs from evil makes himself a prey. Then the Lord saw it, and it displeased Him that there was no justice..." How should these things impact the follower of Jesus Christ? In John 17:16-17, Jesus prayed for His own: "They are not of the world, even as I am not of it. Sanctify them by the truth; your word is truth." Early instruction in Proverbs 23:23 is, "Buy the truth and do not sell it; get wisdom, discipline and understanding." In 1 Corinthians 13:6, our attitude and approach to all things should be, "Love does not delight in evil but rejoices with the truth."

How then shall we live? The answer is given in Ephesians 5:8-10, "For you were once darkness, but now you are light in the Lord. Walk as children of light (for the fruit of the Spirit is in all goodness, righteousness, and truth), finding out what is acceptable to the Lord." Being factual or fallacious - which one best describes and defines you at all times and in all things?

FOR THOUGHT AND REFLECTION:

Is there ever an occasion when it is permissible to not tell all of the truth? If so, when and where?

Someone on the Internet asked the following: Is it appropriate for us to alter the truth, to change history, to manipulate facts in order to communicate things in a more attractive and memorable way? If one chooses to re-write history, why is he/she attempting to do it?

What if speaking the truth to another individual would have a negative impact upon him/her, should one restrict speaking the truth to such a one? Would it be wisest to refrain from speaking any truth at all to a troubled person?

What if a "leader-type" is speaking incorrectly or inaccurately, should you say anything to that person? Should you do it as publicly as the incorrect or inaccurate statement? Should you speak to the individual privately about it? Should you ignore it altogether? Explain your answers.

If you had to make a public statement or teach a class, would you use someone else's material and represent it as your own work product? Would you give proper attribution and name the source?

What is plagiarism? How serious a matter is to plagiarize from another? Does this indicate integrity and honesty in all things? What rational would you employ to justify plagiarizing the material produced by another? What about copyright infringement - is that a violation of law?

"You shall not pervert justice; you shall not show partiality, nor take a bribe, for a bribe blinds the eyes of the wise and twists the words of the righteous. You shall follow what is altogether just, that you may live and inherit the land which the Lord your God is giving you."
Deuteronomy 16:19-20

"Therefore, since we have this ministry,
as we have received mercy, we do not lose heart.
But we have renounced the hidden things of shame,
not walking in craftiness nor handling the word of God deceitfully, but by manifestation of the truth commending ourselves to every man's conscience in the sight of God."
II Corinthians 4:1-2

"For He who would love life and see good days,
let him refrain his tongue from evil, and his lips from speaking deceit. Let him turn away from evil and do good;
let him seek peace and pursue it.
For the eyes of the Lord are on the righteous,
and His ears are open to their prayers;
but the face of the Lord is against those who do evil."
I Peter 3:10-12

11. Living Credibly

How should one purpose to live "Amid The Cultural Chaos" and Cultural Slide that has the tendency, similar to an avalanche, to envelop everyone and everything in its path? Is there a guideline for the twenty-first century "Christian" that will prove to be helpful for those who may experience hardships, persecution and turmoil? Several books in the Bible speak of bondage, captivity, dispersion, persecution and martyrdom. One of them is the Book of Hebrews. The sense of the times in which Jewish believers lived is given in Hebrews 10:32-36 (ASV), "But call to remembrance the former days, in which, after you were enlightened, you endured a great conflict of sufferings; partly, being made a gazing stock both by reproaches and afflictions; and partly, becoming partakers with them that were so used. For you both had compassion on them that were in bonds, and took joyfully the spoiling of you possessions, knowing that you have for yourselves a better possession and an abiding one. Cast not away therefore your boldness, which has great recompense of reward. For you have need of patience, that, having done the will of God, you may receive the promise." The challenge is for the Jewish believers to continue to endure and not cast away their confidence in Jehovah God. Obviously, this has application for all generations of God's people.

The possibility of persecution is very real and is on their immediate horizon. They are weary and discouraged. It is even possible that inwardly they had given thought to abandonment of Christianity and returning to their traditional Judaism. Can one manage to survive at any cost as a follower of Jesus Christ? Is it viable and feasible to consider survival amid chaos and suffering? In reference to the possibility of persecution, they receive these words in Hebrews 12:3-4, "For consider Him who endured such hostility from sinners against Himself, lest you become weary and discouraged in your souls. You have not yet resisted to bloodshed, striving against sin." There is the additional word in Hebrews 10:38, "Now the just shall live by faith; but if anyone draws back, My soul has no pleasure in him." The "just shall live by faith" in this passage is followed by an entire chapter, Hebrews 11, that serves as a Roll Call of those who have dared to live by faith through many challenging and adverse circumstances. The consequence for the one who "draws back" is this word from The Lord: "My soul has no pleasure in him." Consider this statement with the appeal of Ezekiel 18:31-32, "Cast away from you all the transgressions which you have committed, and get yourselves a new heart and a new spirit. For why should you die, O house of Israel? For I have no pleasure in the death of one who dies, says the Lord God. Therefore turn and live!"

    There is a compelling passage near the conclusion of Hebrews 11:32-40 that demonstrates the persistence, perseverance, endurance and confidence of preceding generations of those who dared to follow the Lord wholeheartedly: "And what more shall I say? For the time would fail me to tell of Gideon and Barak and Samson and Jephthah, also of David and Samuel and the prophets: who through faith subdued kingdoms, worked righteousness, obtained promises, stopped the mouths of lions, quenched the violence of fire, escaped the edge of the sword, out of weakness were made strong, became valiant in battle, turned to flight the armies of the aliens. Women received their dead raised to life again. And others were tortured, not accepting deliverance, that they might obtain a better resurrection. Still others had trial of mockings and scourgings, yes, and of chains and imprisonment. They were stoned, they were sawn in two, were tempted, were slain with the sword. They wandered about in sheepskins and goatskins, being destitute, afflicted, tormented - of whom the world was not worthy. They wandered in deserts and mountains, in dens and caves of the earth. And all these, having obtained a good testimony through faith, did not receive the promise, God having provided something better for us, that they should not be made perfect apart from us." One can only wonder regarding how the twenty-first century "Christian" living in the United States of America would embrace and endure under such dire possibilities and hostilities. Could it be said of the 21st Century professing "Christian" – "of whom the world was not worthy"?

What lessons can one learn from The Book of Hebrews regarding how one is to live in the day of uncertainty, confusion and turmoil? Is there a way for one to maintain the faith-course in the midst of a cultural tsunami and ensuing chaos? These few examples from Hebrews indicate what the expectation of any follower of Jesus Christ in any generation or culture should be. In

Hebrews 4, 6, 10-13, there seems to be the use of a mnemonic device (something intended to assist the memory, as a verse or formula). In the Greek New Testament Grammar, it is known as the Hortatory Subjunctive - "a statement urging others to join in some action (commanding oneself and one's associates). It is easily identified because it will always be the first person plural form of the subjunctive mood. This verb form will often come near the beginning of the sentence and is usually translated "let us."

The Hortatory Subjunctive is not just common to the Holy Scriptures but has also been employed in the political arena. There is a political statement made by Samuel Adams near the time of the American Revolution and the Boston Tea Party. While addressing the delegates to the Continental Congress meeting at Yorktown, Pennsylvania in 1777 (quoted in The Life and Public Services of Samuel Adams, Volume 2, by William Vincent Wells; Little, Brown, and Company; Boston, 1865 ; pp. 492-493), he said: "The eyes of the people are upon us... If we despond, public confidence is destroyed, the people will no longer yield their support to a hopeless contest, and American liberty is no more...Despondency becomes not the dignity of our cause, nor the character of those who are its supporters. Let us awaken then, and evince a different spirit - a spirit that shall inspire the people with confidence in themselves and in us - a spirit that will encourage them to persevere in this glorious struggle, until their rights and liberties shall be established on a rock. We have proclaimed to the world our determination 'to die freemen, rather than to live slaves. We have appealed to Heaven for the justice of our cause, and in Heaven we have placed our trust...We shall never be abandoned by Heaven while we act worthy of its aid and protection." The use of the Hortatory Subjunctive in this historical reference is evidenced in the sentence that begins: "Let us awaken then, and evince a different spirit - a spirit that shall inspire the people with confidence." This is comparable to what the writer of Hebrews is seeking to do with the Jewish believers who have been subjected to external pressures and coercions. The "let us" passages serve as an encouragement and inspiration for a harassed and oppressed people. One of the implications of these verses and passages is to remind the people of God that they are not alone in the struggle. There are others of like precious faith who had and are having to persevere amid the pressures and deprivations "Amid The Cultural Chaos."

In the devotional, Today In The Word for September 8th, 2013, the text referenced is Ecclesiastes 4:10, "But woe to him who is alone when he falls, for he has no one to help him up." The devotional states: "...'I've fallen, and I can't get up!' is the tag line for television advertisement for a medical alarm and protection company. The commercial pictures an older woman lying on the floor. She is scared that no one will hear her plea for help. Fortunately, with the medical service, she can speak into a device and talk to those who will send help. Most of us understand this fear of being alone without anyone to help care for us. In this section of Ecclesiastes, Scripture addresses the weaknesses of living in solitude. The passage addresses the problems of oppression and isolation. As Solomon considered oppression in the world, he declares that it would be better for some to have never been born (v. 3). While this pessimistic view of life might seem shocking, it also forces us to recognize the amount of cruelty and evil in this earthly existence…"

This is similar to the sense of solitude expressed by Elijah in I Kings 19:9-10. He has been very ambitious and courageous for the Lord, but then a threat is made by Jezebel against his life. In fear and with battle-fatigue, he runs to escape the threat. Elijah has allowed himself to think that God has forsaken him and left him to cope with his circumstances alone. He has allowed himself to forget that no one can ever run away from the presence of God. Elijah will realize this truth in a dramatic way when he has a moment of confrontation and a reality check with the Lord, Who says to him precisely and personally: "What are you doing here, Elijah? So he (Elijah) said: I have been very zealous for the Lord God of hosts; for the children of Israel have forsaken Your covenant, torn down Your altars, and killed Your prophets with the sword. I alone am left; and they seek to take my life." It seems as though Elijah's frustrations and fears have a tone of accusation toward God when he states: (1) it is "Your Covenant" that has been forsaken; (2) it is "Your Altars" that have been torn down; and (3) it is "Your Prophets" that have been killed – and now – I am here all-alone. It's as though he is responding to God's: "What are you doing here, Elijah?" with - What difference does it make where I am? Everything is disintegrating around me. In actuality, I am the only Prophet left and as soon as they find me, they will kill me. Then You, Lord, will have no one else to represent you as a Prophet. Is Elijah correct in his feelings and conclusions? Does he have an accurate sense of his circumstance as compared with living his life in the presence of God? Why does he continue his reasoning before God while God is speaking with him?

That which he needed and we need to remember are the words recorded in Romans 11:2-5, "God has not cast away His people whom He foreknew. Or do you not know what the Scripture says of Elijah, how he pleads with God against Israel, saying, Lord, they have killed Your prophets and torn down Your altars, and I alone am left, and they seek my life? But what does the divine response say to him? I have reserved for Myself seven thousand men who have not bowed the knee to Baal. Even so then, at this present time there is a remnant according to the election of grace." It validates the point that we are not alone in ministry for the Lord, nor is an individual isolated and ignored by the Lord. We are part of the "let us" because we are part of "a remnant according to the election of grace." There is a danger of an egoism becoming part of one's thinking. When present, it distorts the truth about God and His being in control. It ignores another truth that if His people become silent about Him and His Standards due to opposition, He can cause stones and rocks to speak out. In Luke 19:39-40, "...some of the Pharisees called to Him from the crowd, Teacher, rebuke Your disciples. But He answered and said to them, I tell you that if these should keep silent, the stones would immediately cry out."

As we explore the statements and implications of the "let us" guidance and instruction, we find most of the Hortatory Subjunctives are in Hebrews 10 and 12, although other "let us" references appear in Hebrews 4, 6 and 13. Some of them are very obvious whereas others are implied or inferred. It must be remembered and understood that a faith behavior is being urged upon the readers and hearers. It is a call to conduct oneself in a committed way to a life of faith in Jesus Christ. What are these mnemonic devices and where do the Hortatory Subjunctives appear in Hebrews? The first verses using the "let us" verb form is in Hebrews 4:1, 11, 14, 16 - "Therefore, since a promise remains of entering His rest, let us fear lest any of you seem to have come short of it. Let us therefore be diligent to enter that rest, lest anyone fall according to the same example of disobedience. Seeing then that we have a great High Priest who has passed through the heavens, Jesus the Son of God, let us hold fast our confession. Let us therefore come boldly to the throne of grace, that we may obtain mercy and find grace to help in time of need." The thrust is obvious: (1) "let us" not fall short of the promised eternal rest in Christ; (2) "let us" diligently pursue that path to His rest and not become sidetracked because of disobedience; (3) "let us" hold fast to and maintain our confession and profession of faith by remaining close to and in communication with our Great High Priest, Jesus Christ; and (4) "let us" boldly seek Him and come before Him at His throne of grace where there is always abundant mercy and grace for every child of God who seeks Him and purposes to walk in His ways.

The glue that holds all of this in place and makes it possible is Hebrews 4:15: "For we do not have a High Priest who cannot sympathize with our weaknesses, but was in all points tempted as we are, yet without sin." Our High Priest, Jesus Christ, knows our plight and trials; He is aware of our cares and concerns; He is our Model and Example of the potential and possibility of walking in obedience and fellowship with Him. He resisted temptations (Matthew 4:1-11) and will enable us, by His mercy and grace, to resist them as well (I John 2:15-17). Hebrews 4:15 reminds one that "He was in all points tempted as we are, yet without sin." Regarding the times when temptations cascade upon one and the pressures of the culture weigh heavily, there is a reminder for the children of God to implement that which the "let us" instructs and urges us to do. Jesus reminds His people that He has traveled down the same road we travel. He experienced the temptations, trials and pressures just like we do. He wants us to know – I have been where you are and have been challenged similarly. I want you to know – I've been there and done that, and remained unscathed by the enemy. By My grace, I will help you and be with you - I will never leave you or forsake you.

When temptations and trials come, we have this word in I Corinthians 10:12-13, "Therefore let him who thinks he stands take heed lest he fall. No temptation has overtaken you except such as is common to man; but God is faithful, Who will not allow you to be tempted beyond what you are able, but with the temptation will also make the way of escape, that you may be able to bear it." He has a perfect plan and purpose for each of us (Jeremiah 29:11, Romans 8:28) and will always be with us. What are the ways and means of escape from the temptations one must endure and overcome? Perhaps the most important area is Prayer, especially remembering the words Jesus taught His disciples (Matthew 6:13), "And do not lead us into temptation, but deliver us from the evil one. For Yours is the kingdom and the power and the glory forever." The words of encouragement found in II Peter 2:9 are reassuring, "the Lord knows how to deliver the godly out of temptations." We need to remind ourselves and each other in terms of the importance to "let us" do what God has prescribed in His Word for one's deliverance and spiritual health.

Another lesson to be learned regarding the temptations one experiences is touched upon in John 15:1-11. This passage deals with the vine and the branches. The reality of the passage is that many times it is necessary for the keeper of the vine to prune away that which is non-productive or diseased. The words of Jesus are: "I am the true vine, and My Father is the vinedresser. Every branch in Me that does not bear fruit He takes away; and every branch that bears fruit He prunes, that it may bear more fruit...Abide in Me, and I in you. As the branch cannot bear fruit of itself, unless it abides in the vine, neither can you, unless you abide in Me. I am the vine, you are the branches. He who abides in Me, and I in him, bears much fruit; for without Me you can do nothing. If anyone does not abide in Me, he is cast out as a branch and is withered; and they gather them and throw them into the fire, and they are burned." The idea of the parable pertains to the relationship of the branches to The Vine, as well as the health of the branches so they can be most fruitful and productive. There is a disease that can infiltrate the vine and minimize its effectiveness. Only the vigilant vinedresser is capable of detecting the disease of the branches. It is a disease known as phylloxera. It is "a tiny insect species that becomes a serious pest on plants. Phylloxera form galls on and can defoliate Hickory and Pecan trees, but it has devastating effect with grape vines."

One of the ways phylloxera infiltrates the vine occurs when birds build a nest within the refuge and safety of the vine. If the vine could be humanized, it might even respond that the beautiful birds and the sweet sound of their chirping and song is a welcomed change. The vine was so lonely in its isolation. However, the very thing that was welcomed into the midst of the vine proved to be the carrier of the insect species that will begin to destroy the vine. As painful as it is, the nest must be removed and the affected branches must be cut off and burned. If this is not done, the vine will slowly die. There is a similarity to the disease infiltrating the vine and sin that is allowed to take up residence in one's life. That which appears to be beautiful and lovely is allowed into our lives and becomes a welcomed guest. All seems to be going along well – until – spiritual phylloxera sets in and begins its negative work. The pruning process of removing the spiritual phylloxera can be – and will be painful. However, for one's spiritual health and survival, the pruning must be thoroughly done in order that one may be restored to being fruitful and productive.

Jesus stresses the necessity for being close to The Vinedresser and His wise and necessary pruning that will enable one to be more fruitful. If we bridge and relate this disease to temptation, we can begin to realize how a very small matter can result in a very great consequence. In God's sight there are no small sins and no allowable temptations if the vine is to remain healthy. Just as the phylloxera must be pruned, removed and burned, even so the temptations must not be allowed to remain and become latent in one's life. The chaotic culture would suggest otherwise and try to exert its alternatives upon one. The chaotic culture is part of the disease plague (phylloxera) that will destroy the vine and your life if it is not addressed and prevented from doing so.

In Chapter 10, I referenced God's design and purpose for His people. II Peter 1:3-4, 8 states: "His divine power has given to us all things that pertain to life and godliness, through the knowledge of Him who called us by glory and virtue, by which have been given to us exceedingly great and precious promises, that through these you may be partakers of the divine nature, having escaped the corruption that is in the world through lust... if these things are yours and abound, you will be neither barren nor unfruitful in the knowledge of our Lord Jesus Christ." Phylloxera will prevent the fruitfulness and productivity that is God's desire for His people. It would be foolish to hang onto the bird's nest in our vine and to prefer the lilt of the bird's song even though it would cause us to begin to wither and slowly die. Is it the presence of the nest or the song of the birds that is the cause of the problem? No! It is the "tiny insect species that becomes a serious pest" that will slowly but surely "defoliate" our vine and render us useless and fruitless. It should occasion us to pray the prayer in Psalm 139:23-24, "Search me, O God, and know my heart; try me, and know my anxieties; and see if there is any wicked way in me, and lead me in the way everlasting." The New Living Translation of these verses is: "Search me, O God, and know my heart; test me and know my thoughts. Point out anything in me that offends you, and lead me along the path of everlasting life." The searching process is to uncover the spiritual phylloxera that has been allowed to inhabit my vine and is rendering me fruitless and unproductive. Why is this search and destroy process necessary?

    We receive our answer in another "let us" section is Hebrews 6:1 where a high standard is set before the people of God. The verse states: "Therefore, leaving the discussion of the elementary principles of Christ, let us go on to perfection, not laying again the foundation of repentance from dead works and of faith toward God." As we focus on, "let us go on to perfection," it is addressing the need for one to stay away from anything that would defile and/or prevent one from being all of what God wants one to be. The direction to achieve the goal of perfection is shared in I Thessalonians 4:3-8, "For this is the will of God, your sanctification: that you should abstain from sexual immorality; that each of you should know how to possess his own vessel in sanctification and honor, not in passion of lust, like the Gentiles who do not know God; that no one should take advantage of and defraud his brother in this matter, because the Lord is the avenger of all such, as we also forewarned you and testified. For God did not call us to uncleanness, but in holiness. Therefore he who rejects this does not reject man, but God, who has also given us His Holy Spirit."

Why is it so vital for each of us to transparently deal with the spiritual phylloxera in our lives? Hebrews 12:11-14 assists us with the answer, namely, "Now no chastening seems to be joyful for the present, but painful; nevertheless, afterward it yields the peaceable fruit of righteousness to those who have been trained by it. Therefore strengthen the hands which hang down, and the feeble knees, and make straight paths for your feet, so that what is lame may not be dislocated, but rather be healed. Pursue peace with all people, and holiness, without which no one will see the Lord." The action being required of us to "Pursue peace and holiness." The reason attached to this action is, "without which no one will see the Lord." The prayer one offers from his/her heart might well be the words of a Hymn written by P.P. Bliss (1838-1876): "More holiness give me, More strivings within, More patience in suffering, More sorrow for sin..." If this is the prayer and direction of our lives, we will be involved in the process of: "let us go on to perfection." However, if we ignore this as a personal need and direction, then we will be numbered among those of whom it is said: "without which no one will see the Lord." One will be "A Casualty" rather than "A Conqueror" who lives and serves victoriously.

FOR THOUGHT AND REFLECTION:

If persecution became a reality in our nation, what concerns would you have? Why?

Read Mark 13:7-13. In the midst of the cultural chaos and turmoil in the world, where would one expect to find protection and a safe haven? How will children behave toward their parents and the parents toward their children? What would that mean/cause for you personally, your family, your church and your community? What would happen to basic trust among people?

When Hebrews 4:15 states: "we do not have a High Priest who cannot sympathize with our weaknesses", are you able to identify your "weaknesses"? What would you identify as your greatest weakness?

In regard to "spiritual phylloxera," what are you allowing to take up residence in your life that will affect your spiritual health? Do you allow it because it is pleasurable? Does it occur because you have become lax or careless?

If you are aware of the "spiritual phylloxera," what is the first thing you should do? Are you able to do this on your own or should you seek Heavenly Help to thoroughly deal with this issue in your life?

Would you want John 15:1-11 to be the process in your life even though "pruning" can and will be painful? At the end of the pruning, what awaits one (See: John 15:11)?

"...that which we have seen and heard we declare to you,
that you also may have fellowship with us;
and truly our fellowship is with the Father
and with His Son Jesus Christ."
I John 1:3

"Finally, brethren, whatever things are true, whatever things are noble, whatever things are just, whatever things are pure, whatever things are lovely, whatever things are of good report, if there is any virtue and if there is anything praiseworthy - meditate on these things. The things which you learned and received and heard and saw in me, these do, and the God of peace will be with you."
Philippians 4:8-9

12. Regret or Reward

For many, as they near the end of life, either feel or express regret about some things they have done or not done. By way of reflection, the greater regret falls in the area of what had not been done. Some websites have listed the following report: "An Australian palliative nurse, Bronnie Ware has recorded the top five regrets of the dying on a blog...which was so popular she wrote a book called The Top Five Regrets of The Dying (in the last 12 weeks of their lives): (1) I wish I'd had the courage to live a life true to myself, not the life others expected of me; (2) I wish I hadn't worked so hard; (3) I wish I'd had the courage to express my feelings; (4) I wish I had stayed in touch with my friends; and (5) I wish that I had let myself be happier." One of her observations was: "Many people suppressed their feelings in order to keep peace with others. As a result, they settled for a mediocre existence and never became who they were truly capable of becoming. Many developed illnesses relating to the bitterness and resentment they carried as a result." Another of her observations is: they "...did not realize until the end that happiness is a choice. They had stayed stuck in old patterns and habits. The so-called 'comfort' of familiarity overflowed into their emotions, as well as their physical lives. Fear of change had them pretending to others, and to themselves, that they were content, when deep within, they longed to laugh properly and have silliness in their life again."

An attachment to the above is: "So the blue print for a life with less regret is clear: (1) Forget what others think... start living your passion today and understand the great value and freedom health affords you today...choices. So make some now! (2) Men especially enjoy more time with your family and less with the boss, working harder is no guarantee of success, slow down, think smarter and redefine success as options not things; (3) Express your feelings and become who you are truly capable of becoming; (4) Get in touch with friends who have enriched your life and lock in a time to have fun together regularly; (5) Happiness is a choice not a destination claim yours back today!" One can only wonder if any of those with regrets had any affiliation within a spiritual setting. If they did, how did they miss knowing about the rewards benefit rather than the regrets experience and reality? How many of these people make a statement that they hope they are going to heaven but lack any relationship to Jesus Christ and the assurance that ensues from one's knowing and obeying Him? How many will die in and with their regrets without ever knowing the peace, forgiveness and joy rewards that belong exclusively to those who belong to Jesus Christ? How many should have been informed of Hebrews 11:6, "But without faith it is impossible to please Him, for he who comes to God must believe that He is, and that He is a rewarder of those who diligently seek Him"? The operative words of blessing and encouragement in this paragraph are: "He is a rewarder."

While the above two paragraphs are primarily a secular statement, there is value in gleaning some of the applicable truths to the spiritual commitments that a follower of Christ should know and do. The "let us" commitment in the Book of Hebrews enlightens one in terms of life-choices and the benefit that can be received by doing them. When they are prayerfully considered, one will readily discern the distinction between the regrets and rewards factors. The prevailing question would be: Do you want your life to be one that is filled with regrets or one that is overflowing with rewards? Hebrews 10:19-25 instructs the follower of Jesus Christ, "Therefore, brethren, having boldness to enter the Holiest by the blood of Jesus, by a new and living way which He consecrated for us, through the veil, that is, His flesh, and having a High Priest over the house of God, let us draw near with a true heart in full assurance of faith, having our hearts sprinkled from an evil conscience and our bodies washed with pure water. Let us hold fast the confession of our hope without wavering, for He who promised is faithful. And let us consider one another in order to stir up love and good works, not forsaking the assembling of ourselves together, as is the manner of some, but exhorting one another, and so much the more as you see the Day approaching."

The above passage contains three direct "let us" references and two that are inferred or implied. The first "let us" statement is: "let us draw near with a true heart in full assurance of faith, having our hearts sprinkled from an evil conscience and our bodies washed with pure water." There is "a High Priest over the house of God" (Jesus Christ), and we are to be aware of Him and the need for drawing near to Him at all times. Initially, the way one becomes positioned to be drawing near to the High Priest is established in John 6:37, 44. "All that the Father gives Me will come to Me, and the one who comes to Me I will by no means cast out. No one can come to Me unless the Father who sent Me draws him; and I will raise him up at the last day." The Father is engaged in drawing people to the Son where the oneness-in-Christ relationship is established with the reward being: (a) I will not cast him out and (b) I will raise him up at the last day. Is this your assurance and hope - or - will you approach physical death with regrets rather than anticipation of the rewards reserved for those who diligently believe in and follow Christ?

The second "let us" statement is: "Let us hold fast the confession of our hope without wavering, for He who promised is faithful. The "confession" is something other than a creedal or doctrinal subscription. It is something other than the practice of entering a booth and telling someone your faults, short-comings and perceived sins. The "confession" being referenced should include at least Romans 10:8-10, 13 – "The word is near you, in your mouth and in your heart" (that is, the word of faith which we preach): that if you confess with your mouth the Lord Jesus and believe in your heart that God has raised Him from the dead, you will be saved. For with the heart one believes unto righteousness, and with the mouth confession is made unto salvation...For whoever calls on the name of the Lord shall be saved."

The basis for one's "confession of hope" depends upon one's relationship to Jesus Christ. When that becomes the reality, there is a basis for the hope that it is the "confession...made unto salvation."

Any confession made unto salvation must include the acknowledgement and admission of sin. A study of I John will assist one in realizing, recognizing and repenting of sin. I John 1:9 states plainly: "If we confess our sins, He is faithful and just to forgive us our sins and to cleanse us from all unrighteousness." I John 4:15-16 emphasizes, "Whoever confesses that Jesus is the Son of God, God abides in him, and he in God. And we have known and believed the love that God has for us. God is love, and he who abides in love abides in God and God in him." Years ago, an appeal often employed by the itinerant evangelist was: "Keep short accounts with God." Their application was: "Don't delay in dealing with and confessing sin. Get right with God, now!" The idea was to speak to the urgency of the moment and to respond to the Gospel without any further delay. The succinctness and simplicity of the Gospel is stated in I John 5:11-13, "And this is the testimony: that God has given us eternal life, and this life is in His Son. He who has the Son has life; he who does not have the Son of God does not have life. These things I have written to you who believe in the name of the Son of God, that you may know that you have eternal life, and that you may continue to believe in the name of the Son of God." Is this your confession of hope today? We need to maintain a firm grip on the promises of God to His people in His Word. This basic truth and principle is vital and very important so that one will come to know and believe that God always keeps His Word.

There is another place for confession of sin and that is within the body of believers known as "the church." In James 5:14-16, we read: "Is anyone among you sick? Let him call for the elders of the church, and let them pray over him, anointing him with oil in the name of the Lord. And the prayer of faith will save the sick, and the Lord will raise him up. And if he has committed sins, he will be forgiven. Confess your trespasses to one another, and pray for one another, that you may be healed. The effective, fervent prayer of a righteous man avails much." That which seems so necessary and obvious to do is often met with resistance or reluctance. Some reasons given are: (1) this is a private matter between me and the Lord; (2) if I confess my faults to the elders, they will tell their wives, who in turn will share it with their friends, and then my good name will be besmirched; and (3) this is too embarrassing to share with those who are not confessing their sins and their faults. There are situations where those who are supposed to minister in the name of Christ are not united together as servants of the Lord. There was a church that was having internal differences and a group of godly men asked the leaders of that church if they would be willing to go to a room and reconcile their differences on the basis of James 5:16. Even though it seemed like a reasonable request, those leaders decided to vote on it. The result of their vote was one-half of the leaders voted to try it and one-half voted to refuse to try it. The sad result was that the internal impasse continued.

One man offered the rationale of "his group" by allowing that it would only cause trouble if it was done. His rationale was never explained. The question, however, remained: "How can the application of Biblical principle not be beneficial?"

A devotional shared regarding carnality with "the church" quoted I Corinthians 3:1-3, "And I, brethren, could not speak to you as to spiritual people but as to carnal, as to babes in Christ. I fed you with milk and not with solid food; for until now you were not able to receive it, and even now you are still not able; for you are still carnal. For where there are envy, strife, and divisions among you, are you not carnal and behaving like mere men?" The thought expressed contained reference to a fact that the Lord's people ought to be a sanctified, pure, clean people. However, too often there is carnality in attitude, in taste and in many things. A suggested personalized prayer would be: Deliver me from carnal attitudes, actions, and desires. Search, purify and cleanse me. I want to live with the awareness of Your presence with me. I want to begin to take a serious God seriously. Amen. These are words one would do well to heed and a prayer one would do well to pray.

The third "let us" statement is: "let us consider one another in order to stir up love and good works, not forsaking the assembling of ourselves together, as is the manner of some, but exhorting one another, and so much the more as you see the Day approaching." Truths that serve as a reminder of the authority and faithfulness of God appear throughout the Holy Scriptures. We, along with God's people in all generations, are reminded in Deuteronomy 31:6, "Be strong and of good courage, do not fear nor be afraid for the Lord your God, He is the One who goes with you. He will not leave you nor forsake you." Additionally, in Zephaniah 3:17, is this word about where God constant relationship with His people, "The Lord your God in your midst, The Mighty One, will save; He will rejoice over you with gladness, He will quiet you with His love, He will rejoice over you with singing." There is another reminder of what the Lord does in behalf of His people stated in I Corinthians 10:13, "No temptation has overtaken you except such as is common to man; but God is faithful, who will not allow you to be tempted beyond what you are able, but with the temptation will also make the way of escape, that you may be able to bear it." The Lord makes His completeness available to all who faithfully follow Him.

Within Hebrews 10:24 are two additional implied "let us" statements: (a) "let us" not forsake the assembling of ourselves together, and (b) "let us" be exhorting one another, and so much more as we see the Day approaching. "To stir up love and good works" would seem like the logical outcome of one who has committed his/her life to Jesus Christ. The question remains, are we accomplishing this task regarding love and good deeds, or has the effort failed along the way? In your relationship within the "church", has anyone impacted your life in terms of the love and good deeds principle? As the culture exerts more of its influence upon our society, it is also having an impact on the thinking and dedication of many within the context of "the church"! It must be understood that "the love and good deeds" spoken of here is an outgrowth of one's salvation. It is not a means of achieving it. It is part of the edification process enabling one to become more and more like Christ and less and less of self. Hopefully, this is something that you've experienced and are regularly exercising.

Regarding the instruction - "let us" not forsake the assembling of ourselves together - many studies have been done over the past generation about the pattern and participation in church attendance. A uniform conclusion is that church attendance is showing a steady decline so that on a given Lord's Day less than twenty percent of the members are in attendance for a worship service. The conclusions regarding why this is the trend are basically uniform as well (in researching this topic, most use the same survey work of two resources, namely, A Gallup Poll and the data assembled by the Evangelical Free Church). It should also be noted that the surveys focused on the major recognized orthodox religious groups. If you became part of a survey sample about church attendance, what would you say are three of the major reasons for the decline in attendance? If it became personalized and you were asked about your own church attendance view and the influence your view has had on your family, where would you/they be included and numbered in the survey?

Within the church culture, from a classical to a contemporary view, there are many varied thoughts about the form, function and purpose of the Church universal as well as the

Church particular. The Lord's design and purpose for His Church is clearly stated and defined. In Ephesians 4:11-16, "And He Himself gave some to be apostles, some prophets, some evangelists, and some pastors and teachers, for the equipping of the saints for the work of ministry, for the edifying of the body of Christ, till we all come to the unity of the faith and of the knowledge of the Son of God, to a perfect man, to the measure of the stature of the fullness of Christ; that we should no longer be children, tossed to and fro and carried about with every wind of doctrine, by the trickery of men, in the cunning craftiness of deceitful plotting, but, speaking the truth in love, may grow up in all things into Him who is the head – Christ - from whom the whole body, joined and knit together by what every joint supplies, according to the effective working by which every part does its share, causes growth of the body for the edifying of itself in love."

To this end, there is a necessary organization and structure. An example of this is shared in Acts 15:1-6 where a Church Council came together to consider a conflict that had arisen, "And certain men came down from Judea and taught the brethren, unless you are circumcised according to the custom of Moses, you cannot be saved. Therefore, when Paul and Barnabas had no small dissension and dispute with them, they determined that Paul and Barnabas and certain others of them should go up to Jerusalem, to the apostles and elders, about this question...And when they had come to Jerusalem, they were received by the church and the apostles and the elders; and they reported all things that God had done with them. But some of the sect of the Pharisees who believed rose up, saying, it is necessary to circumcise them, and to command them to keep the Law of Moses. Now the apostles and elders came together to consider this matter." After they had pondered the variant views, and prayed for God's wisdom, they arrived at their decision and determination. The letter they sent to the people in the Church is simple and is recorded in Acts 15:22-29, "Then it pleased the apostles and elders, with the whole church, to send chosen men of their own company to Antioch with Paul and Barnabas, namely, Judas...and ...wrote this letter by them: The apostles, the elders, and the brethren, to the brethren who are of the Gentiles in Antioch, Syria, and Cilicia: Greetings. Since we have heard that some who went out from us have troubled you with words, unsettling your souls, saying, You must be circumcised and keep the law - to whom we gave no such commandment - it seemed good to us, being assembled with one accord, to send chosen men to you...men who have risked their lives for the name of our Lord Jesus Christ...For it seemed good to the Holy Spirit, and to us, to lay upon you no greater burden than these necessary things: that you abstain from things offered to idols...and from sexual immorality. If you keep yourselves from these, you will do well."

It is somewhat intriguing to see the complications that arise within particular churches. Some of them occur as a result of a person (or group of persons) exerting a personal strong will and/or a self-interpretation of a Biblical passage make that a binding rule to be applied to the people within the church. Some are oriented to the preservation traditions and rituals, rather than allowing for the "new creation" work by God's love, mercy and grace. The above response by the Apostles and Elders maintains a focus on that which is basic and stated in Scripture. The Church today should try to focus on the things that unite the body of Christ rather than those things that can and will cause diversity and/or division.

FOR THOUGHT AND REFLECTION:

If/When you reflect upon your life within the body of believers – the Church, are there things for which you sense considerable regret?

If it was possible for you to be able to have a "do-over" on sections of your life, what are some things you would "do-over" differently?

Do you believe there is a right and proper place for confessing some sins, faults and personal matters to others? If so, would it be on the basis that "confession is good for the soul" or because it is the way in which the body of believers is supposed to function?

If you were able to make changes in terms of the form, function and purpose of the local church you attend, what are some of them you would make? State why you would make your changes!

Have you ever attempted to invest your life in that of another for the purpose of edification (or mentoring) "according to the effective working by which every part does its share, causes growth of the body for the edifying of itself in love."? What was the result of your effort?

The Prayer of the Lord Jesus Christ for His People – The Church:

"But now I come to You, and these things I speak in the world, that they may have My joy fulfilled in themselves. I have given them Your word; and the world has hated them because they are not of the world, just as I am not of the world. I do not pray that You should take them out of the world, but that You should keep them from the evil one. They are not of the world, just as I am not of the world. Sanctify them by Your truth. Your word is truth. As You sent Me into the world, I also have sent them into the world. And for their sakes I sanctify Myself, that they also may be sanctified by the truth. I do not pray for these alone, but also for those who will believe in Me through their word; that they all may be one, as You, Father, are in Me, and I in You; that they also may be one in Us, that the world may believe that You sent Me. And the glory which You gave Me I have given them, that they may be one just as We are one: I in them, and You in Me; that they may be made perfect in one, and that the world may know that You have sent Me, and have loved them as You have loved Me."
John 17:13-23

13. Stirred and Focused

Chapter 12 considered Hebrews 10:24, "And let us consider one another in order to stir up love and good works." One can too easily become absorbed with the minutia of life and miss out on the opportunities to become involved in the lives and spiritual needs of others. If the focus is shifted off of Jesus Christ, one can become discouraged and disgruntled in the journey through life. As a result, the opportunity "to stir up love and good works" gets lost as an individual attempts to cope with his/her personal duties, concerns and pressures of life. "Amid The Cultural Chaos" as on attempts to survive the many uncertainties of life, these uncertainties may contribute to a spiritual malaise (a vague or unfocused of mental uneasiness, or lethargy) within one. It can/will easily sideline one from focusing on and doing the priorities of life and ministry. Jesus cautioned His followers regarding their focus and disciplines in life when He said in the parable of the seed and the sower (Matthew 13:22): "Now he who received seed among the thorns is he who hears the word, and the cares of this world and the deceitfulness of riches choke the word, and he becomes unfruitful." When this is allowed to occur, "to stir up love and good works" is sacrificed and forgotten.

In a devotional by Dr. Adrian Rogers entitled, "Be An Encourager", he writes about the contrast between the discourager and the encourager: "Someone has well said that discouragement is a dark room where the negatives of fear and failure are developed…" He goes on to include a series of Action Points: (1) Find a needy person and enrich him; (2) Find a lonely person and include him; (3) Find a misunderstood person and affirm him; (4) Find an undiscovered person and develop him; and (5) Find a failing person and restore him. These Action Points can serve to stir up the individual so he/she can regain both focus and traction as we implement God's Word in our own life and make it known for implementation in the lives of others. Our lives need to be lived away from the weeds and thorns in the world. In this way, The Seed of the Word will be received by fertile soil and will be productive to the benefit of many.

The Hortatory Subjunctive ("let us" references and inferences) continue in Hebrews 12 and 13. They pick up on the theme that illustrate both how and why one can persevere and reach the finish line – not somehow – but triumphantly. Reaching the goal - not as "A Casualty" – but as "A Conqueror". Looking at the accomplishment, not as a victim but as a victor. Hebrews 12:1-3 tells us how we are to run toward the finish line. It will require discipline and perseverance. Those who are cited as having finished the course well are cheering us on in Hebrews 12:1, "Therefore…since we are surrounded by so great a cloud of witnesses." Who are these "cloud of witnesses"?

It is a hackneyed recommendation in Scriptural exposition that whenever one sees a "therefore" the question one should ask is what/why is it there-for? In this passage, it seems obvious that the "therefore" requires returning to Hebrews 11 and being reminded of those who have preceded us on this life-journey and the race toward the finish line. The chapter reminds us of those who have persevered and have been commended for their faith in the midst of many challenges, obstacles, hardships and limitations. They serve as "witnesses" to and for us as we travel down a similar path "Amid The Cultural Chaos" and ongoing uncertainty. The witnesses shout out to us to keep on going. They are assuring us that we can finish this race just as they did. The victor's crown is not awarded to the faint-hearted or to those who grew weary and quit. It is awarded to those who have persevered and finished the race – not somehow, but triumphantly.

To that end, there are eight behavioral guidelines and rules that will determine the way we will finish the course set before us. They include: (1) "let us" not become encumbered with sin. It is difficult to imagine seeing a runner in a race carrying suitcases and having a back-pack strapped on. Any observer with common sense would opine that the runner has been ill-advised in terms of what is required to successfully run the race. Such an entrant would soon learn that he/she is incapable of enduring the rigor of the race; (2) "let us" run with endurance. The skilled and determined runner knows that he/she must exercise good judgment when it comes to personal baggage. The obvious choice is to turn loose of the baggage and enter the race unencumbered. In this way, one will be enabled to run with greater endurance. While it is nice to hear the cheers from the witnesses, it is better still to be focused on Jesus: (3) "let us" look unto Jesus in and for all things. There is a beautiful scene and illustration of looking to Jesus as Stephen approaches the finish line in Acts 7:54-59, "...they gnashed at him with their teeth. But he, being full of the Holy Spirit, gazed into heaven and saw the glory of God, and Jesus standing at the right hand of God, and said, Look! I see the heavens opened and the Son of Man standing at the right hand of God! Then they cried out with a loud voice, stopped their ears, and ran at him with one accord; and they cast him out of the city and stoned him...they stoned Stephen as he was calling on God and saying, Lord Jesus, receive my spirit."

Why was Stephen able to endure what he did? How was he able to maintain a correct focus amid the rage and threats of men? How could he maintain his composure when he knew his faithful testimony and witness would result in his death? The answer is because of his knowledge of The Word and his commitment to it. It enabled him to implement: (4) "let us" pay attention to all of what Jesus suffered and endured. In the opening Chapters of The Book of Acts, both Peter and Stephen gave a courageous witness and message to those who surrounded them. On their part, there was a readiness and willingness to be completely identified with Jesus Christ. They remembered the words of Jesus during His earthly ministry (Luke 9:22-23), "The Son of Man must suffer many things, and be rejected by the elders and chief priests and scribes, and be killed, and be raised the third day. Then He said to them all: If anyone desires to come after Me, let him deny himself, and take up his cross daily, and follow Me." The obvious commitment of Stephen was to be that kind of man and person for Jesus Christ.

As one continues as a participant in the race marked out before us, there are other areas to be cared for and maintained. These behaviors and pursuits are continued in Hebrews 12:14-15. One must be careful to be among those who are committed to: (5) "let us" pursue peace and the things that make for peace. The only way we can accomplish this behavior and goal for life is through receiving what Jesus has left us and given us. In John 14:27, Jesus has left us peace and given us peace. In John 16:33, Jesus knows the context of our lives and the difficulties we will face. Despite that, Jesus states: "These things I have spoken to you, that in Me you may have peace. In the world you will have tribulation; but be of good cheer, I have overcome the world."

There is never time afforded to us during the race (or battle) where we can retreat to the sidelines and attempt to rest, recuperate or retire. There are particulars in the life of a follower of Christ that are a work and process. With this being the case, a child of God can assert that he/she is a work in process. This is applicable when we are directed to: (6) "let us" pursue holiness because it is the pathway to seeing the Lord. The words are cogent: "Pursue peace with all people, and holiness, without which no one will see the Lord." It is interesting that peace and holiness are linked together. It is also compelling to realize their significance with God because His Word states: "...without which no one will see the Lord." We must be mindful to heed the words of II Corinthians 7:1, "... having these promises, beloved, let us cleanse ourselves from all filthiness of the flesh and spirit, perfecting holiness in the fear of God." The follower of Christ is to pursue holiness and perfect holiness in fear of God. The idea of "fear" includes being in His presence with awe and reverence. There is no place for flippancy or matter-of-factness in His presence. As we live the Christian life and maintain a spiritual posture and walk "Amid The Cultural Chaos", we must always maintain the sense of awe and reverence before Him. As we proceed in the race set before us, we should also remember that we are who and what we are because of the love, mercy and grace of our God.

The Lord expects His children to obey Him and to live by His Standards without exception. He leaves one no room to compromise: (7) "let us" carefully live our lives and guard against any root of bitterness springing up that can and will cause trouble and/or defilement. Why is the "root of bitterness" significant for those who are running the race that is marked out before us? There is a basic and important reason given in this regard in Ephesians 4:30-32, "And do not grieve the Holy Spirit of God, by whom you were sealed for the day of redemption. Let all bitterness, wrath, anger, clamor, and evil speaking be put away from you, with all malice. And be kind to one another, tenderhearted, forgiving one another, just as God in Christ forgave you." The first thing mentioned that grieves the Spirit of God is bitterness. Matthew Henry comments on this passage: "By bitterness, wrath, and anger, are meant violent inward resentment and displeasure against others: and, by clamor, big words, loud threatening, and other intemperate speeches, by which bitterness, wrath, and anger, vent themselves. Christians should not entertain these vile passions in their hearts." A Dictionary definition of bitterness is: "strong, unrelenting hostility or resentment; difficult or unpleasant to accept; cutting and sarcastic." Matthew George Easton in his Illustrated Bible Dictionary states about: "Bitterness is symbolical of affliction, misery, and servitude (Exodus 1:14 ; Ruth 1:20 ; Jeremiah 9:15). The Chaldeans are called the 'bitter and hasty nation' (Habakkuk 1:6). The "gall of bitterness" expresses a state of great wickedness (Acts 8:23). A 'root of bitterness' is a wicked person or a dangerous sin (Hebrews 12:15)."

One additional Hortatory Subjunctive appears in Hebrews 12:28, (8) "let us" have grace that will enable one to serve God acceptably with reverence and godly fear. Whenever one pauses to worship the Lord, whether in private or public, it should be viewed as a special time of offering to God all that will exalt and honor His Name. Many of the Psalms indicate ways in which one can come to worship the Lord. It is always a time that is to be marked by reverence and godly fear and it includes what the "let us" is to do and how it can be done. Why is this to be one's approach in coming to God? An apt response is Psalm 95:6-7, "Oh come, let us worship and bow down; let us kneel before the Lord our Maker. For He is our God, and we are the people of His pasture, and the sheep of His hand." Earlier in the Psalm (verses 1-3); The Psalmist indicates how one is privileged to come into the presence of God (we should notice his use and application of "let us"): "Oh come, let us sing to the Lord! Let us shout joyfully to the Rock of our salvation. Let us come before His presence with thanksgiving; Let us shout joyfully to Him with psalms. For the Lord is the great God, and the great King above all gods."

Another picture of Worship is given in Isaiah 6:1-5. The prophet shares his vision: "...I saw the Lord sitting on a throne, high and lifted up, and the train of His robe filled the temple. Above it stood seraphim; each one had six wings: with two he covered his face, with two he covered his feet, and with two he flew. And one cried to another and said: Holy, holy, holy is the Lord of hosts; the whole earth is full of His glory! ...So I said: Woe is me, for I am undone! Because I am a man of unclean lips, and I dwell in the midst of a people of unclean lips; for my eyes have seen the King, The Lord of hosts." This is very similar to a scene of Worship given in Revelation 4:8-11, "The four living creatures...do not rest day or night, saying: Holy, holy, holy, Lord God Almighty, Who was and is and is to come! Whenever the living creatures give glory and honor and thanks to Him who sits on the throne, who lives forever and ever, the twenty-four elders fall down before Him who sits on the throne and worship Him who lives forever and ever, and cast their crowns before the throne, saying: You are worthy, O Lord, To receive glory and honor and power; for You created all things, and by Your will they exist and were created." In both passages, Isaiah 6 and Revelation 4, the reality of reverence and godly fear is seen. The things that are not present or seen are any form of entertainment or jocularity when coming before the Lord. It is a time for serious contemplation about the greatness and holiness of God. Psalm 150 instructs what can be melodically utilized in the worship of God. The Psalmist wrote: "Praise the Lord! Praise God in His sanctuary; Praise Him in His mighty firmament! Praise Him for His mighty acts; Praise Him according to His excellent greatness! Praise Him with the sound of the trumpet; Praise Him with the lute and harp! Praise Him with the timbrel and dance; Praise Him with stringed instruments and flutes! Praise Him with loud cymbals; Praise Him with clashing cymbals! Let everything that has breath praise the Lord. Praise the Lord!" While the Psalm speaks of various instruments that can be used, it stresses that the focus is to be Praise to the Lord. It should never be interpreted as an entertainment form or a performance that results in applause being given to a person. Whatever sound emanates from the instruments, it must always fit into the required reverence and godly fear.

Worship also requires integrity as one approaches God. There is no room or place for deceit, hypocrisy, Pharisaism or dishonesty. There are two examples that illustrate the need for integrity in worship, especially as it pertains to what is being offered to God and what the worshippers are representing it to be. The first illustration is Joshua 7:1, 10-14 (ASV). But the children of Israel committed a trespass in the devoted thing; for Achan...took of the devoted thing: and the anger of Jehovah was kindled against the children of Israel. And Jehovah said unto

Joshua, Get thee up; wherefore art thou thus fallen upon thy face? Israel hath sinned; they have even transgressed my covenant which I commanded them: they have even taken of the devoted thing, and they have even put it among their own stuff. Therefore the children of Israel cannot stand before their enemies; they turn their backs before their enemies, because they are become accursed: I will not be with you any more, except ye destroy the devoted thing from among you. Up, sanctify the people, and say, Sanctify yourselves against tomorrow: for thus says Jehovah, the God of Israel, There is a devoted thing in the midst of thee, O Israel; thou canst not stand before your enemies, until ye take away the devoted thing from among you. In the morning therefore you shall be brought nearby your tribes: and it shall be, that he that is taken with the devoted thing shall be burnt with fire, he and all that he hath; because he hath transgressed the covenant of Jehovah, and because he hath wrought folly in Israel." The entire nation stood on the threshold of extinction because one person lacked integrity when it came to reverence and godly fear before the Lord. The sin and sinner would have to be purged and the rest of the nation would have to be sanctified if they had any hope of survival and conquering the Promised Land.

The second illustration is given in Acts 5:1-11, "But a certain man named Ananias, with Sapphira his wife, sold a possession. And he kept back part of the proceeds, his wife also being aware of it, and brought a certain part and laid it at the apostles' feet. But Peter said, Ananias, why has Satan filled your heart to lie to the Holy Spirit and keep back part of the price of the land for yourself? While it remained, was it not your own? And after it was sold, was it not in your own control? Why have you conceived this thing in your heart? You have not lied to men but to God. Then Ananias, hearing these words, fell down and breathed his last. So great fear came upon all those who heard these things..." People were selling land and possessions so there would be adequate supply for the work of the emerging church. For whatever reason, Ananias made a decision to give only a portion of the proceeds of the sale, even though he had made a commitment to give all. Peter states the indictment: "Why has Satan filled your heart to lie to the Holy Spirit and keep back part of the price of the land for yourself?" The judgment was swift and the people witnessed God striking him dead. How did the people respond when they witnessed God's wrath and judgment upon Ananias? The summary is: "So great fear came upon all those who heard these things." However, Sapphira his wife was complicit in this lie. Three hours later, when she is confronted about her participation in this deception, the same judgment of God becomes her plight. The response among the people was similar (verse 11): "So great fear came upon all the church and upon all who heard these things."

The manner in which one worships the Lord and that which one brings to the Lord are part of the act in approaching Him with reverence and godly fear. God never has pleasure in/with irreverence, frivolity or second-rate worship. In Malachi 1:6-10, there is a complaint that God brings against His people,

He asks and answers: "A son honors his father and a servant his master. If then I am the Father, where is My honor? And if I am a Master, where is My reverence? says the Lord of hosts to you priests who despise My name. Yet you say: In what way have we despised Your name? You offer defiled food on My altar. But say, In what way have we defiled You? By saying, The table of the Lord is contemptible. And when you offer the blind as a sacrifice, Is it not evil? And when you offer the lame and sick, Is it not evil? Offer it then to your governor! Would he be pleased with you? Would he accept you favorably? Says the Lord of hosts. But now entreat God's favor, that He may be gracious to us. While this is being done by your hands, will He accept you favorably?" says the Lord of hosts. Who is there even among you who would shut the doors, so that you would not kindle fire on My altar in vain? I have no pleasure in you, says the Lord of hosts, nor will I accept an offering from your hands." There is a continuance of the complaint in terms of the tithes and offerings that were being given to the Lord. In Malachi 3:8-10, God is speaking and says: "Will a man rob God? Yet you have robbed Me! But you say, In what way have we robbed You? In tithes and offerings. You are cursed with a curse, for you have robbed Me, Even this whole nation. Bring all the tithes into the storehouse, that there may be food in My house, and try Me now in this, says the Lord of hosts, if I will not open for you the windows of heaven and pour out for you such blessing that there will not be room enough to receive it."

The gravity of these complaints is seen in the words of the Lord when He states: "I have no pleasure in you!" Again, when He asks the rhetorical question: "Will a man rob God? Yet you have robbed Me!" Once again, it is a deliberate act by a person to come to God on personal rather than Biblical terms. God is responding that it isn't the worship He requires or accepts, nor are the sacrifices and gifts offered meaningful to Him. He wants His people to come before Him reverently and with godly fear. He wants His people to be enthusiastic and generous in their giving to Him, They should never skimp or cut corners when they worship and give to The Almighty God.

When people gather for a Worship Service, it should not be viewed as just another social activity but a special time of corporate focus upon God and worship of Him. We need to block out the cultural chaos and news of the day. It is not a time for matter-of-factness or frivolity. It is a time when we come before The Holy God Who is to be the sole object of our focus and Who is receiving our offering of Worship. The Psalmist would remind us of how we are to approach God: (1) Let us sing to the Lord! (2) Let us shout joyfully to the Rock of our salvation! (3) Let us come before His presence with thanksgiving! (4) Let us shout joyfully to Him with psalms! We are to do this because: "... the Lord is the great God, and the great King above all gods." To expand on this, Paul would write in Colossians 3:16-17, "Let the word of Christ dwell in you richly in all wisdom, teaching and admonishing one another in psalms and hymns and spiritual songs, singing with grace in your hearts to the Lord. And whatever you do in word or deed, do all in the name of the Lord Jesus, giving thanks to God the Father through Him." Corporately, we are to enthusiastically worship our God and to be involved in building up one another in and as we worship Him.

FOR THOUGHT AND REFLECTION:

Do you view yourself as a person who encourages and builds others up? Are you more detached than involved with your brothers and sisters in Christ?

How well do you think you have run or are running the race that is marked out for you? Are there things, of which you are aware, that hinder you and hold you back – maybe even sidelining you? What should you do about that? When should it be done?

In this Chapter, eight behavioral guidelines and rules were listed. Of these eight guidelines/rules, which one(s) need the most attention in your life and the life of the church you attend? Are these guidelines/rules appropriate and necessary for application within a local church?

If you selected two of them as the beginning point for church renewal, which ones would you select? Why?

How seriously should one embrace and implement the words: "Pursue peace with all people, and holiness, without which no one will see the Lord."? Is this something that is done occasionally or should it be on a continual process? Within one's life, as well as in a local church, how will this be evidenced?

In terms of integrity in Worship, a statement was made in this Chapter – "There is no room or place for deceit, hypocrisy, Pharisaism or dishonesty." Pharisaism is defined as: "rigid observance of external forms of religion or conduct without genuine piety." If a person or church is failing to take a serious God seriously, how should this behavior and activity be defined? What should be done to correct such an approach?

This Chapter also touched upon "bitterness" and the impact it can have in an individual's life, as well as in a particular church? Is "bitterness" ever justified? If so, when and why? How does the Holy Spirit see and respond to any form of bitterness (See: Ephesians 4:30)?

WORSHIP WITH AWE, REVERENCE, FEAR
Oh come; Let us sing to the Lord!
Let us come before His presence with thanksgiving...
For the Lord is the great God...
Oh come, let us worship and bow down;
Let us kneel before the Lord our Maker.
For He is our God.
Psalm 95 (Selected)

14. What's Next?

The trends in our nation, world and culture have similarity to those of other nations in other historical times. In both the Old and New Testaments of Holy Scripture, many instances of captivity, enslavement, oppression and suppression, and religious persecution are indicated. One of the best and most succinct summaries of the History of Persecution appears in The International Standard Bible Encyclopedia (ISBE - 1915) where the following is stated: "The importance of this subject may be indicated by the fact of the frequency of its occurrence, both in the Old Testament and New Testament where in the King James Version the words persecute, persecuted, persecuting are found no fewer than 53 times, persecution 14 times, and persecutor 9 times. ISBE cites the words of Jesus in Matthew 23:34-36, "Therefore, indeed, I send you prophets, wise men, and scribes: some of them you will kill and crucify, and some of them you will scourge in your synagogues and persecute from city to city, that on you may come all the righteous blood shed on the earth, from the blood of righteous Abel to the blood of Zechariah...whom you murdered between the temple and the altar. Assuredly, I say to you, all these things will come upon this generation..." They go on to cite the summary words recorded in Hebrews 11:36-38, "Still others had trial of mocking and scourging, yes, and of chains and imprisonment. They were stoned, they were sawn in two, they were tempted, and they were slain with the sword.

They wandered about in sheepskins and goatskins, being destitute, afflicted, tormented - of whom the world was not worthy. They wandered in deserts and mountains, in dens and caves of the earth."

ISBE also mentions the various forms of persecution that would be utilized: "The methods of persecution which were employed by the Jews, and also by the heathen against the followers of Christ, included: (1) Men would revile them and would say all manner of evil against them falsely, for Christ's sake (Matthew 5:11). (2) Contempt and disparagement: "Say we not well that thou art a Samaritan, and hast a demon?" (John 8:48). "If they have called the master of the house Beelzebub, how much more them of his household!" (Matthew 10:25). (3) Being, solely on account of their loyalty to Christ, forcibly separated from the company and the society of others, and expelled from the synagogues or other assemblies for the worship of God: "Blessed are ye, when men shall hate you, and when they shall separate you from their company, and reproach you, and cast out your name as evil, for the Son of man's sake" (Luke 6:22); "They shall put you out of the synagogues" (John 16:2). (4) Illegal arrest and spoliation of goods, and death itself. All these various methods, used by the persecutor, were foretold, and all came to pass. It was the fear of apprehension and death that led the eleven disciples to forsake Jesus in Gethsemane and to flee for their lives. Jesus often forewarned them of the severity of the persecution which they would need to encounter if they were loyal to Him: "They will put you out of the synagogues; yes, the time is coming that whoever kills you will think that he offers God service. (John 16:2); "I send you prophets, wise men, and scribes: some of them you will kill and crucify, and some of them you will scourge in your synagogues and persecute from city to city..." (Matthew 23:34).

How can our generation expect to be exempt from any form or type of persecution? How much longer will we be able to freely worship without fear of hostile opposition interrupting the public gathering? How much longer can we expect to openly exercise our religious preferences without government control? We must remember that we are a nation that has little or no room for God in the public arena and discourse. There is restriction placed on Bible Reading, Prayer (especially if one should close by saying: "in Jesus' Name") and reference to anything religious in a classroom setting (particularly if it is from a Judeo-Christian perspective). God's Laws are flaunted and His Word is ignored. Any mention of a God-standard, if it pertains to abortion and same-gender unions, is rejected and scorned. The Gay Rights movement even has the audacity to interrupt political discourse to champion their partner-preferences and rights. In that regard, the legislators who passed these laws, hoping to increase their voter base, have opened the proverbial Pandora's Box that will not be easily closed or sealed.

In the midst of an emerging and eroding culture that is becoming more and more radical, as well as chaotic, how is the church to minister and how is the follower of Christ to live? Speaking to some of the ills of our nation and culture, Peggy

Noonan shared some of her thoughts on "Work and the American Character" (August 30, 2013): "...I've been thinking about the big bad stories of the summer, the cultural ones that disturb people. The sick New York politician who, without apparent qualms, foists his sickness into the public sphere again. The kids who kill the World War II vet because they're bored. The kids who kill the young man visiting from Australia because they too are bored, and unhappy, and unwell. The teacher who has the affair with the 14-year-old student, and gets a slap on the wrist from the judge. The state legislator who's a sexual predator, the thieving city councilor and sure, the young pop star who is so lewd, so mindlessly vulgar and ugly on the awards show. We're shocked. But we're not shocked. And that itself is disturbing. We're used to all this, now, this crassness and lowness of public behavior. The cumulative effect of these stories, I suspect, is that we're starting to fear: Maybe that's us. Maybe that's who we are now. As if these aren't separate and discrete crimes and scandals but a daily bubbling up of the national character..." Is Peggy Noonan correct about the possibilities of the national character? What about the Judeo-Christian influence, values and foundation – have they been completely eradicated and/or obliterated from the fiber and character of the nation? In the midst of this emerging and eroding chaotic culture, how is the church to minister and how is the follower of Christ to live? Can there be a positive voice both raised and heard amid the din of secularism? Can the Church and the Christian begin to be light in a world and culture that is becoming increasingly more comfortable in the midst of haziness and darkness?

There are interesting elements of this answer given in Hebrews 10 through 12. Hebrews 10 has given guidelines and rules by which the Christian and The Church is to live and function; Hebrews 11 stresses the need for and examples of faith – that it can be implemented and viable in many varied circumstances. It underscores in (Hebrews 11:6) that "...without faith it is impossible to please Him, for he who comes to God must believe that He is, and that He is a rewarder of those who diligently seek Him." Hebrews 12 addresses the race before us and the challenges of pursuing the finish line and goal. The advantage belongs to those who keep on looking to Jesus (Hebrews 12:2). There is emphasis that one should persevere and not give up. In 1890, Fanny Crosby wrote a Refrain for the Hymn, Victory Through Grace. These words should echo from within us as we run the race and endeavor to be an adequate servant and representative of our Lord: "Not to the strong is the battle, Not to the swift is the race, Yet to the true and the faithful - Victory is promised through grace."

Hebrews 13 emphasizes what one is to do despite all hardships, persecutions or challenges to one's faith. Regardless of any or all of the external happenings and circumstances, the Christian and the Church are to maintain stability before the Lord. He is their life and message. One of the hortatory subjunctives – the "let us" passage - is Hebrews 13:12-13 where the instruction and identification factor is given: "Therefore Jesus also, that He might sanctify the people with His own blood, suffered outside the gate. Therefore let us go forth to Him, outside the camp, bearing His reproach." The operative phrases are: (1) Jesus suffered outside the gate; (2) He did this to sanctify a people unto Himself; (3) We are to go outside to be identified with Him; (4) We, too, will bear His reproach with Him. This testifies to the fact that the Christian and the Church is unashamed to know Jesus Christ and of making Him known. It will also reflect that both the individual and corporate body are taking a serious God seriously, and handling and implementing the Word of God responsibly and seriously.

This identification with and relationship to Jesus Christ has an additional "let us" step in Hebrews 13:15-16, "Therefore by Him let us continually offer the sacrifice of praise to God, that is, the fruit of our lips, giving thanks to His name. But do not forget to do good and to share, for with such sacrifices God is well pleased." The idea of sacrifice should be part of who we are as a child of God. What is the sacrifice suggesting? Are we to be making sacrifices to God today? If so, what are they and when are they to be offered? Our response and focus will be upon three passages of Scripture.

The first aspect of sacrifice is in Romans 12:1, "I beseech you therefore, brethren, by the mercies of God, that you present your bodies a living sacrifice, holy, acceptable to God, which is your reasonable service." The emphasis is obvious - "your bodies a living sacrifice." The J.B. Phillips translation of Romans 12:1-2 is, " With eyes wide open to the mercies of God, I beg you, my brothers, as an act of intelligent worship, to give him your bodies, as a living sacrifice, consecrated to him and acceptable by him. Don't let the world around you squeeze you into its own mold, but let God re-mold your minds from within, so that you may prove in practice that the plan of God for you is good, meets all his demands and moves towards the goal of true maturity."

A second aspect of sacrifice is indicated in Philippians 4:18, "Indeed I have all and abound. I am full, having received from Epaphroditus the things sent from you, a sweet-smelling aroma, an acceptable sacrifice, well pleasing to God." It involves one's willingness and readiness to share with others in a tangible way. When we do so, that act is construed as being an act of reverence toward God; it becomes "a sweet-smelling aroma" in the nostrils of God and is, and is considered as "an acceptable sacrifice" offered to Him. In this area, we would do well to examine and be reminded of the words in James 2:14-16, "What does it profit, my brethren, if someone says he has faith but does not have works? Can faith save him? If a brother or sister is naked and destitute of daily food, and one of you says to them, Depart in peace, be warmed and filled, but you do not give them the things which are needed for the body, what does it profit? Thus also faith by itself, if it does not have works, is dead." We need to be willing to sacrifice in tangible ways with those who are experiencing hardship and economic need.

The practice of offering an acceptable sacrifice to God in a practical way entails one having a compassionate, sensitive and caring heart regarding the well-being of others. It is true that one cannot meet the real needs of everyone. However, each one can and should be available to help and assist someone. What is happening in this day is that there is not just chaos unfolding before us but also a callousness and indifference toward others who have genuine cares and needs. We need to incorporate the words of Hebrews 13:1-3 as we view and respond to our world and culture: "Let brotherly love continue. Do not forget to entertain strangers, for by so doing some have unwittingly entertained angels. Remember the prisoners as if chained with them--those who are mistreated--since you yourselves are in the body also..." While this has direct implication for involvement with brothers and sisters in Christ, it also has application for use with one's acquaintances, neighbors, or strangers we may observe or with whom we may interact. Why should the child of God be concerned and involved? Hebrews 13:16 indicates the reason: "But do not forget to do good and to share, for with such sacrifices God is well pleased." These words should settle the matter for us. Our goal in life should be to do that which pleases God. The question remains: Will it make a difference in how we think and what we are ready and willing to do? If not now – when? If not here – where?

The third aspect of sacrifice and hortatory subjunctive – "let us" - is mentioned in Hebrews 13:15, "Therefore by Him let us continually offer the sacrifice of praise to God, that is, the fruit of our lips, giving thanks to His name." The clarity of what is meant by these words is simple and overpowering – a sacrifice of praise to God; the fruit of our lips; and giving thanks to His name.

It gives one pause to think about whether or not our approach to God is one of praise and thankfulness or one of complaint and discontent for what we think we need. Further, it also gives us pause in terms of the fruit of our lips. Are our lips always used in a positive approach to God to please Him? Are our lips used negatively, sometimes carelessly and thoughtlessly as one engages in gossip, words of bitterness and anger, or stooping to the profanities that our culture uses so casually? The manner in which one gives thanks is a measure of one's heart-gratitude for God's care and provision for one each day. It is also an indication of one's level of reverence toward a Holy God Whom we are to worship and serve with enthusiasm and eagerness.

    Let us reflect on how one can best offer a sacrifice of praise to God. How does one do it? What should one include in such a sacrifice of praise? A couple of illustrations and examples for this include a tradition of Judaism. At a set time in the year, Hallel Psalms – Praise to Jehovah - are sung or repeated. Hallel consists of six Psalms (113-118), which are said as a unit, on joyous occasions, when the praise of God is particularly appropriate…These chapters are expressions of joy and faith in God, and of gratitude for salvation and deliverance from enemies. They were singled out for inclusion in Hallel because they contain the following fundamental themes of the faith of Judaism: the Exodus, the Law of God given at Mount Sinai, and the vastness of God's mercy in all generations…" In the Treasury of David, Charles Haddon Spurgeon's Commentary on the Book of Psalms, he offers these moving and comprehensive thoughts on

Psalm 118:25, "Save now, I beseech thee, O Lord. Hosanna! Let the Son of David live forever; let his saving help go forth throughout all nations. This was the peculiar shout of the feast of tabernacles; and so long as we dwell here below in these tabernacles of clay we cannot do better than use the same cry. Perpetually let us pray that our glorious King may work salvation in the midst of the earth. We plead also for ourselves that the Lord would save us, deliver us, and continue to sanctify us. This we ask with great earnestness, beseeching it of Jehovah. Prayer should always be an entreating and beseeching. O Lord...Let the church be built up: through the salvation of sinners may the number of the saints be increased; through the preservation of saints may the church be strengthened, continued, beautified, and perfected. Our Lord Jesus himself pleads for the salvation and the prosperity of his chosen; as our Intercessor before the throne he asks that the heavenly Father would save and keep those who were of old committed to his charge, and cause them to be one through the indwelling Spirit,"

Another section of Hallel – Praise to God - Psalms is found in Psalms 145-150. They begin with a title of Praise and that word is frequent throughout these Psalms. A good response for why one should be eager to offer praise is given in Psalm 147:1, "Praise the Lord! For it is good to sing praises to our God; for it is pleasant, and praise is beautiful." Praise is to be offered to God through spoken word, song and instrumentality. It is to be exuberant, gleeful and frequent. No one should ever be too busy or weary to offer praise to the Lord. Do you enjoy the times and moments when you can praise the Lord? Do you find the giving, or sacrifice of praise to be both pleasant and beautiful as you do it?

The prayer or benediction given in Hebrews 13:20-21 is likewise beautiful and compelling: "Now may the God of peace who brought up our Lord Jesus from the dead, that great Shepherd of the sheep, through the blood of the everlasting covenant, make you complete in every good work to do His will, working in you what is well pleasing in His sight, through Jesus Christ, to whom be glory forever and ever. Amen." Especially meaningful are the words "…make you complete in every good work to do His will, working in you what is well pleasing in His sight…" It reminds one of the words of Paul in Philippians 1:6, "being confident of this very thing, that He who has begun a good work in you will complete it until the day of Jesus Christ…" and Philippians 2:13, "for it is God who works in you both to will and to do for His good pleasure…" What a joy it is to know that God is working in and through us to bring us to completion – his design and purpose for us. Lest one be tempted to think this is a passive activity or experience, be reminded of the words in Philippians 2:12, "Therefore, my beloved, as you have always obeyed, not as in my presence only, but now much more in my absence, work out your own salvation with fear and trembling…" We are not designed to become a spiritual robot where we expect that God is going to get done what He wants done regardless of what one chooses to do or not do. This is a totally wrong way to think and respond. The Message Paraphrase has this rendering if verse 12, "What I'm getting at, friends, is that you should simply keep on doing what you've done from the beginning. When I was living among you, you lived in responsive obedience. Now that I'm separated from you, keep it up. Better yet, redouble your efforts. Be energetic in your life of salvation, reverent and sensitive before God. These words should be the way we are thinking and doing as God is bringing us to completion – being one who is eagerly engaged within the responsibilities and opportunities afforded us by our God and Savior. We need to remember that no follower of Jesus Christ is ever exempt or excused from involvement in the work God wants to complete in us and through us.

FOR THOUGHT AND REFLECTION:

Do you have any thoughts regarding persecution and whether or not you might face it in some form during your lifetime? Do you think you should be exempt from being maligned, persecuted, or martyred? Explain your response.

Reference was made above to character. How do you define the essentials that constitute Christian Character? Can we expect a secular culture to agree with and practice that which comprises Christian Character? Why? How?

What are your thoughts regarding Worship, offering of Praise to God, and ministering good to those who need care and attention as a Sacrifice To God? What would be your beginning point for any sacrifice of any sort being offered to God? Do you agree that

God has obligated you/us to make a sacrifice or sacrifices to Him? Explain.

Would we do well to return to a tradition of annually using Hallel Psalms 113-118 and 145-150.? How extensively should the church community celebrate – moderately or extravagantly?

In terms of being or becoming complete in Christ, in what ways is one incomplete? What would be changed about us or within us as this process of completeness takes place? Is II Corinthians 5:17 the beginning point? When does one arrive at the fully complete stage of this process?

Devotionally, there are words of a Hymn, of which I am fond. It was written in 1851 by Aaron R. Wolfe and gives a brief summary of the completeness of God's work in and for us, The Hymn title is, Complete In Thee, and some of the stanzas contain these words:

Complete in Thee! No work of mine
May take, dear Lord, the place of Thine;
Thy blood hath pardon bought for me,
And I am now complete in Thee.
Complete in Thee! No more shall sin,
Thy grace hath conquered, reign within;
Thy voice shall bid the tempter flee,
And I shall stand complete in Thee.
Complete in Thee—each want supplied,
And no good thing to me denied;
Since Thou my portion, Lord, wilt be,
I ask no more, complete in Thee.

About the Author

I, the third of three children, was born in Brooklyn, New York and lived the first 20 years of my life there. In late Spring and Summer of 1954, I volunteered to be a worker at Lakeside Bible Conference in Carmel, New York. During the Summer, I met several people who were already in a Bible College or preparing to enter their Freshman year. I stayed in a two man cabin with a man who was President of the Student Body at Columbia Bible College (now Columbia International University) in Columbia, South Carolina. We had been assigned to work with teenagers from New York City. He was in charge of the entire Teen Camp and I worked with the teenaged boys. During the course of the summer, he would frequently ask me whether or not I had ever thought about what God's will and plan for my life might be. His question "bugged" me and I did my best to avoid him and the question.

At the end of the summer, some friends who had pre-enrolled at Columbia Bible College invited me to ride to South Carolina with them and then to hitch-hike back home. I had no other plans and decided to go. Just to "kill time" I sat in the Orientation Sessions with them. I declined to receive the orientation sheets that were being distributed and a Staff Member asked me "Why?" I indicated that I was not a student and had not enrolled – and my plan was to hitchhike back to New York once the classes began. In a very gentle way, they indicated that if I was willing to enroll, they would pray with and for me that God would provide all that was needed so I could attend the Bible College. As I thought about this suggestion, I decided to do what they had suggested and enrolled as a College Freshman. I not only received an excellent Biblical Education but in the Spring Semester (1955) one of the entering female students from Signal Mountain, Tennessee arrived. Although I knew nothing about her, I was immediately attracted to her. In the Spring, there was an Annual Open House tour in the men's dormitories. It was a formal affair and the men and their dates would have dinner together and then tour the men's campus and buildings. I asked this pretty woman from Tennessee, Peggy Ann Fry, if she had been invited by anyone yet. She indicated that she hadn't and agreed to be my "date" for that evening. One date led to another and our relationship was growing. We dated each week thereafter and would usually walk to a large Sears and Roebuck Store. At that time, they had a large furniture department and it afforded us an opportunity to share our likes or dislikes as we walked around the store. Before returning for the Fall 1955 semester, I expressed my love for Peggy and presented her an engagement ring. I asked her to marry me. She was in agreement and said yes. In the providence of God, we became husband and wife in June 1956.

In 1958, I transferred to a new Presbyterian school, Covenant College in St. Louis, Missouri (now located on Lookout Mountain, Georgia). After graduation in 1960, I enrolled in Covenant Theological Seminary and completed my studies there in 1964. After graduation, I was called and served as Pastor, and have served various churches in that capacity for almost 50 years. In one Pastorate, I met a young man who now owns and operates

The Theocentric Publishing Group. Approximately five years ago, he urged me to put into book format some of the things I had learned and taught over the years. I did so and the two most recent books published by Theocentric Publishing Group are: *Practical Awareness of Living In The Presence of God*, and *Taking A Serious God Seriously*. All of the titles authored by me are available on Amazon.

I appreciate your purchase and reading of Amid The Cultural Chaos. I trust it has been beneficial for you and contributed positively to your personal world and life view.

www.ingramcontent.com/pod-product-compliance
Lightning Source LLC
Chambersburg PA
CBHW061637040426
42446CB00010B/1461